Le Festin d'Ésope

and Other Works for Solo Piano

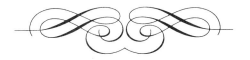

Charles-Valentin
ALKAN

Selected and with Introductory Notes by
MARC-ANDRÉ HAMELIN

DOVER PUBLICATIONS, INC.
Mineola, New York

Bibliographical Note

Charles-Valentin Alkan's piano works were originally published in separate volumes by Richault, Paris [n.d.] [ca. 1857] under the group title *Oeuvres pour le Piano de C:V:Alkan aîné,* later reissued as *Oeuvres choisies pour Piano de Ch. V. Alkan / Edition revue par F. M. Delaborde et I. Philipp* by Fonds Costallat-Billaudot/Editions M.-R. Braun, Paris, n.d. Some works in the series were issued under the related imprint of Gérard Billaudot, Paris, or of Costallat et Cie., Paris [both, n.d.].

This Dover edition, first published in 1998, is a new compilation of six Alkan works originally published separately in this series. "Symphonie," "Concerto," and "Le Festin d'Ésope" are parts of Alkan's *Douze Études dans tous les tons mineurs,* Op. 39. *Saltarelle,* Op. 23, and *Toccatina en ut mineur,* Op. 75, appeared as individual works. "Barcarolle" is the sixth of a collection originally published as *Six Chants,* Op. 65 *(Trente Chants/Troisième Suite)* [1861?].

These six works were selected for this compilation by Marc-André Hamelin, whose Introduction and Notes were specially prepared for the Dover edition. A composite list of contents and main headings are newly added. The footnote on p. 71 is a new English translation of the original French note.

International Standard Book Number: 0-486-40066-2

CONTENTS

The first three works are from *Douze Études dans tous les tons mineurs,* Op. 39
(Twelve studies in all the minor keys, 1857)

Introduction   *vii*
Notes   *ix*

Symphonie.   1
   Op. 39, Nos. 4–7

      (1st part)   Allegro   2
      (2nd part)   *Marche funèbre:* Andantino   20
      (3rd part)   Menuet   26
      (4th part)   *Finale:* Presto   36

Concerto.   53
   Op. 39, Nos. 8–10

      (1st part)   Allegro assai   54
      (2nd part)   Adagio   126
      (3rd part)   Allegretto alla barbaresca   144

Le Festin d'Ésope (Aesop's Feast)   175
   Op. 39, No. 12

      Theme and 25 Variations   176

Saltarelle   203
   Op. 23 (1844)

Barcarolle.   215
   Op. 65, No. 6 (ca. 1844)

      From *Troisième Recueil de Chants* (Third Collection of Songs)

Toccatina   218
   Op. 75 (ca. 1872)

INTRODUCTION

It is hard to believe that the music of Charles-Valentin Alkan has had so long to wait for what little attention it is now getting. This is an immensely impressive body of work—thoroughly innovative, deeply communicative, surprising at every turn—a major achievement of its time and ours, and fully worthy of comparison with the work of the great 19th century masters.

That Alkan was an irresistible force of nature has been clear to recent generations of pianists who championed his long-neglected music. One thinks of Egon Petri, Eduard Erdmann, Harold Bauer, Claudio Arrau, Ronald Smith and—most influentially, for his legendary 1964 Alkan publication, now out-of-print—the late master Raymond Lewenthal. From the concerts, recordings and writings of these artists came a degree of recognition to counter the near-anonymity triggered by the composer himself. His stunning withdrawal from 19th century Parisian society at the moment of possible recognition (bitter, it is said, at having been passed over for an important musical appointment) no doubt contributed as much as any factor to his loss of public stature among better-known contemporaries.

Alkan's music—particularly such large-scale works as his 1857 masterpiece, the *Douze Études dans tous les tons mineurs,* Op. 39—is generally associated with a daunting level of virtuosity and expressive demands, even in its 19th century context. The formidable work of Paganini and Liszt of course comes to mind, somewhat comparable in difficulty but, particularly in the case of Paganini, rarely close to Alkan's imaginative structures, bold tonal experimentation, harmonic daring and compositional control, especially in his greatly extended works.

This is exceptional work by one of the more enigmatic figures in musical history, the severe and puzzling man Busoni ranked with Chopin, Schumann, Liszt and Brahms as "the greatest of the post-Beethoven piano composers."

Marc-André Hamelin
Winter 1998

NOTES

The three large works in this volume are excerpted from Alkan's monumental *Douze Études dans tous les tons mineurs,* Op. 38 (Twelve studies in all the minor keys). Although 19th century piano recitals are known to have stretched to lengths unimaginable today, it is unlikely that Alkan would have expected a complete performance of this opus. Each of its major components—the *Symphony,* the *Concerto,* and *Le Festin d'Ésope*—while an integrated work within itself, is organically unrelated to the other compositions. This aside, a consecutive performance would have been a daunting endurance feat for both performer and audience!

Upon first hearing the *Symphony* or the *Concerto,* the outer layer of instrumental flamboyance tends to obscure the distinctive attributes of these works. Alkan's unique handling of orchestral textures at the piano, for instance, is of a scope, quality and fidelity not encountered even in Liszt's legendary transcriptions. Alkan's textures tend to be thicker and of a timbral quality more faithful to the orchestral model.

Then there is the startling feature of *length,* nowhere more apparent than in the first movement of the *Concerto*—a perfectly structured sonata-allegro stretched to some twenty-eight minutes! So secure is Alkan's mastery of proportioning musical forms, even to such ultra-extensions, that he allows himself a few subtle twists along the way: the frequent contrasts of mood and changes of texture in the development section of this movement (helped along by iron-clad modulatory schemes), and the two strangely beautiful chorale-like interruptions shortly before the extended repeated-note section (pp. 109–110).

The *Symphony*—more concise than the *Concerto,* perhaps less overwhelming on first hearing, and uniting the strongest elements of Alkan's writing—is a wonderful introduction to the composer's world. All four movements are strongly characterized and vastly appealing. The work is distinctive, original and ferociously demanding in its immensely effective keyboard translation of orchestral sonorities. Alkan's dry wit (much more evident outside of Op. 39) makes occasional appearances: notice, for example, how the transition from the trio of the craggy minuet to the beginning of the movement (p. 32) couldn't possibly be more abrupt (in fact, there is none!). By the nobility and power of its ideas the *Symphony* is easily comparable, in this writer's opinion, to the best of Chopin's and Schumann's larger works.

There is really nothing like *Le Festin d'Ésope* (Aesop's Feast) in the entire piano literature. A nine-minute theme-and-variations, it presents a bewildering proliferation of ideas within its tight framework, clothing a simple eight-measure theme in marvelously different and unorthodox ways throughout twenty-five variations.

The title of the work apparently refers to a banquet which Aesop is said to have prepared for his master Xanthus, choosing to base all of its dishes on a single type of food—beef tongue, for this particular meal. Raymond Lewenthal's delightful notes to his Alkan edition took us a step further, suggesting that each variation might represent a different animal in Aesop's fables, "although the composer leaves us free to guess which is which" . . . a decided invitation to imagine all manner of things!

Our edition concludes with three short works: the *Saltarelle,* Op. 23; *Barcarolle,* from Op. 65; and *Toccatina,* Op. 75. The outer pieces are of the *moto perpetuo* mold—manically energetic in the *Saltarelle,* delicately humorous in the *Toccatina* (especially in the insistently repetitious left-hand part of its middle section).

With its modest technical demands, the *Barcarolle* is an ideal introduction to Alkan for most pianists. Taken from his *Troisième Recueil de Chants* (Third Collection of Songs)—inspired by Mendelssohn's *Songs Without Words*—it is one of Alkan's loveliest creations, demonstrating his ability to create intense moods with the simplest of means. And it must be agreed that the bluesy cross-relations in the *maggiore* section (pp. 215–216) are decades ahead of their time!

●

Alkan's metronome markings are to be taken seriously, even when the music seems too fast; they are accurate reflections of the music's character. Anything slower (in fast tempos) is a disservice to the music, affecting flow and structure.

Finally, the unwary reader should approach Alkan's notation with the greatest care. It is all too easy to misread his often-bewildering accidentals, and come to the most astonishing (and incorrect) conclusions! The watchword for the uninitiated is most definitely "Eyes open!"

M.-A. H.

MARC-ANDRÉ HAMELIN studied in his native Montreal before emigrating to the United States in 1980. His international concert career and extensive recording activity— including more than twenty solo-piano CDs issued over the past decade—have earned high critical praise, particularly for his signature performances of Alkan and the complete piano sonatas of both Alexander Scriabin and Nikolai Medtner.

Le Festin d'Ésope
and Other Works for Solo Piano

Symphonie
for Solo Piano

Op. 39, Nos. 4–7

(1857)

1st Part
ALLEGRO (Op. 39, No. 4)

2nd Part
MARCHE FUNÈBRE (Op. 39, No. 5)

Andantino (88 = ♪)

3rd Part
MENUET (Op. 39, No. 6)

34   *Symphonie* (3rd Part)

4th Part
FINALE (Op. 39, No. 7)

Presto (96 = 𝅝)

Concerto
for Solo Piano

Op. 39, Nos. 8-10

(1857)

1st Part
(Op. 39, No. 8)

If one wants to create a concert piece of a suitable length from this Etude, play the adjoining four measures, then go to the sign 𝄍 on [page 111: *A tempo, con brio*]; this, I think, will be the best cut to establish.

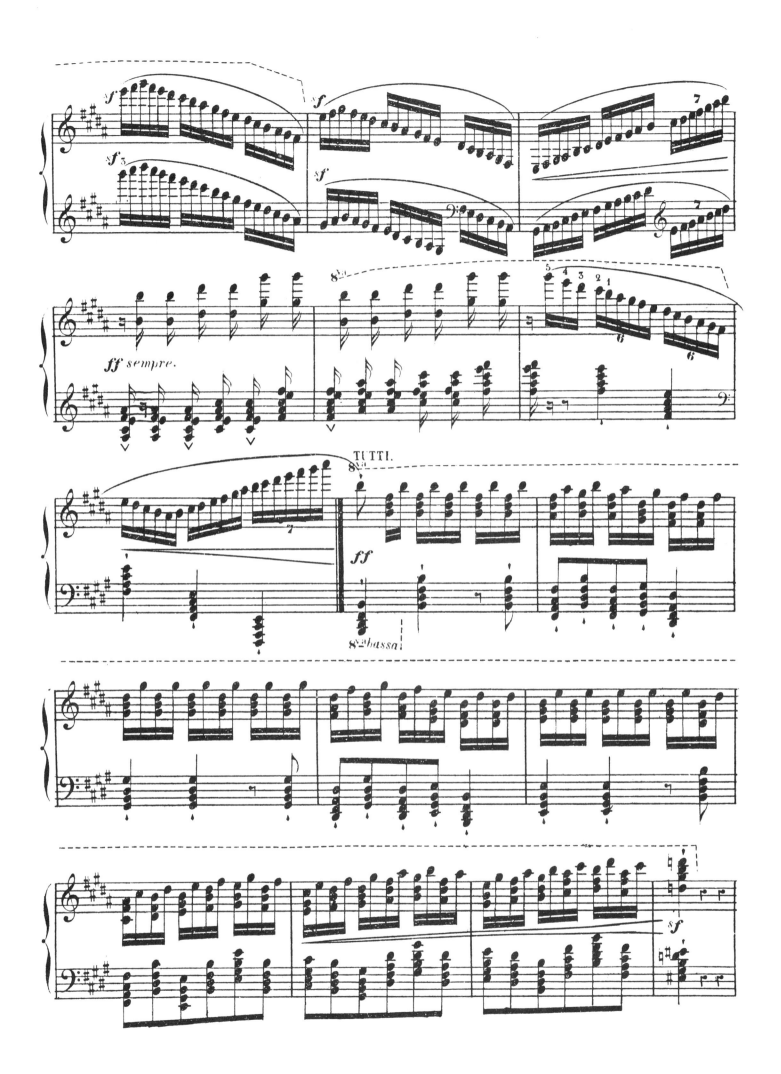

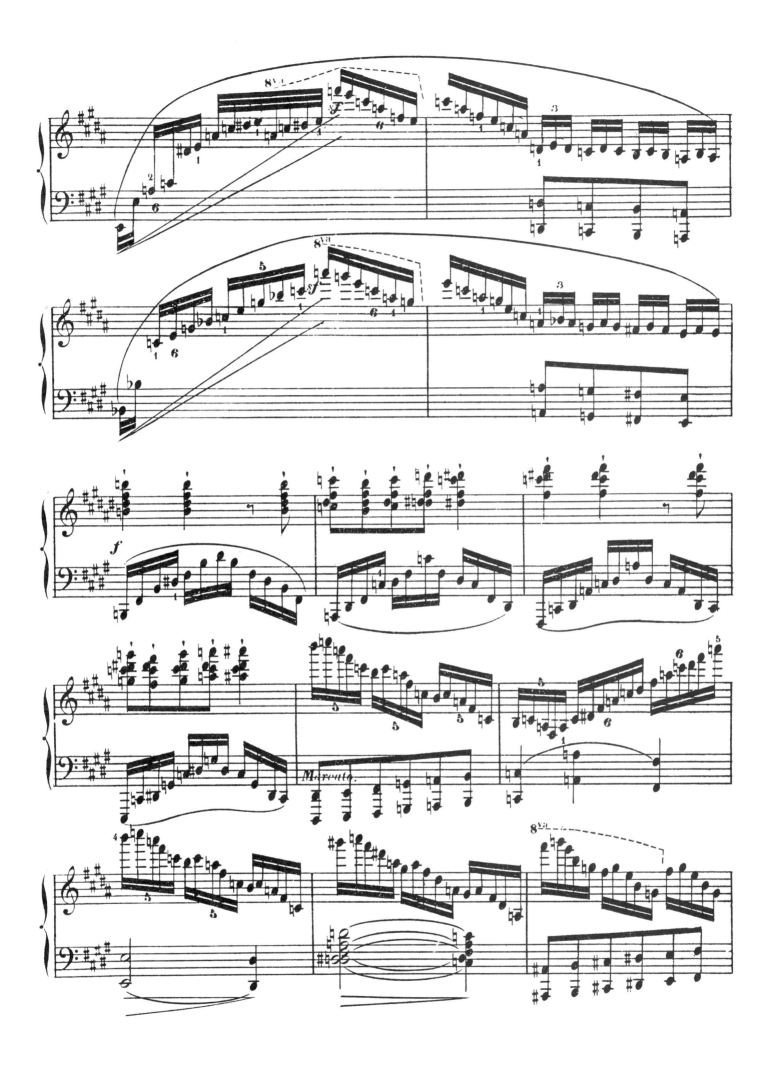

84   *Concerto* (1st Part)

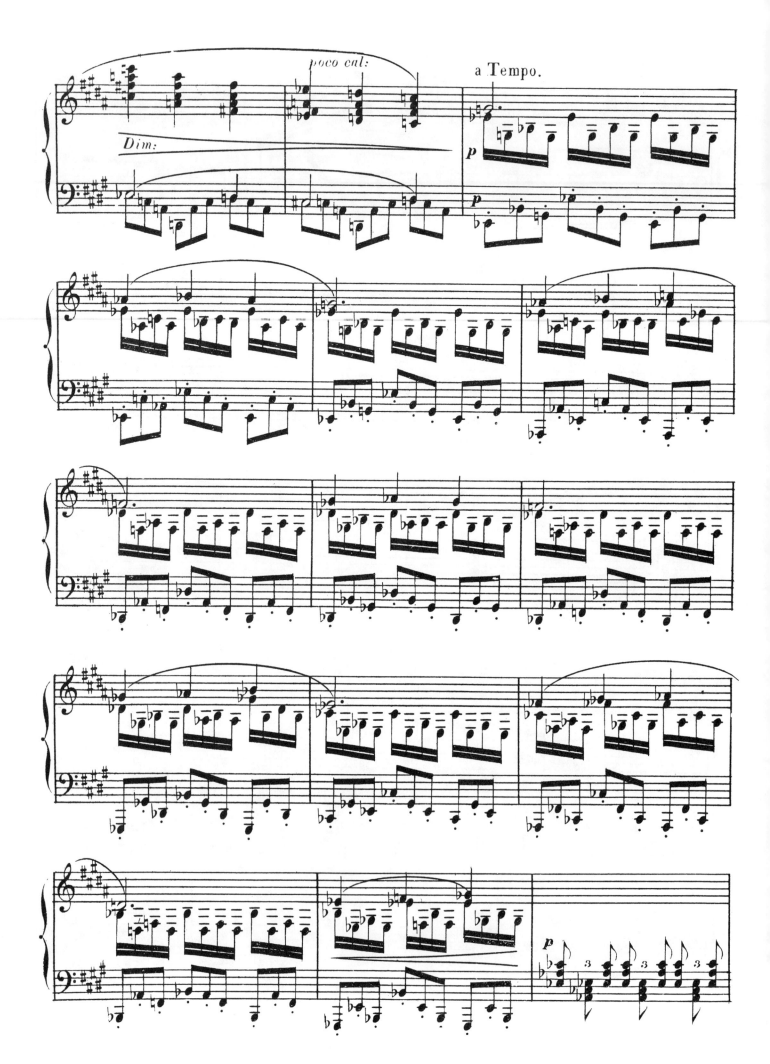

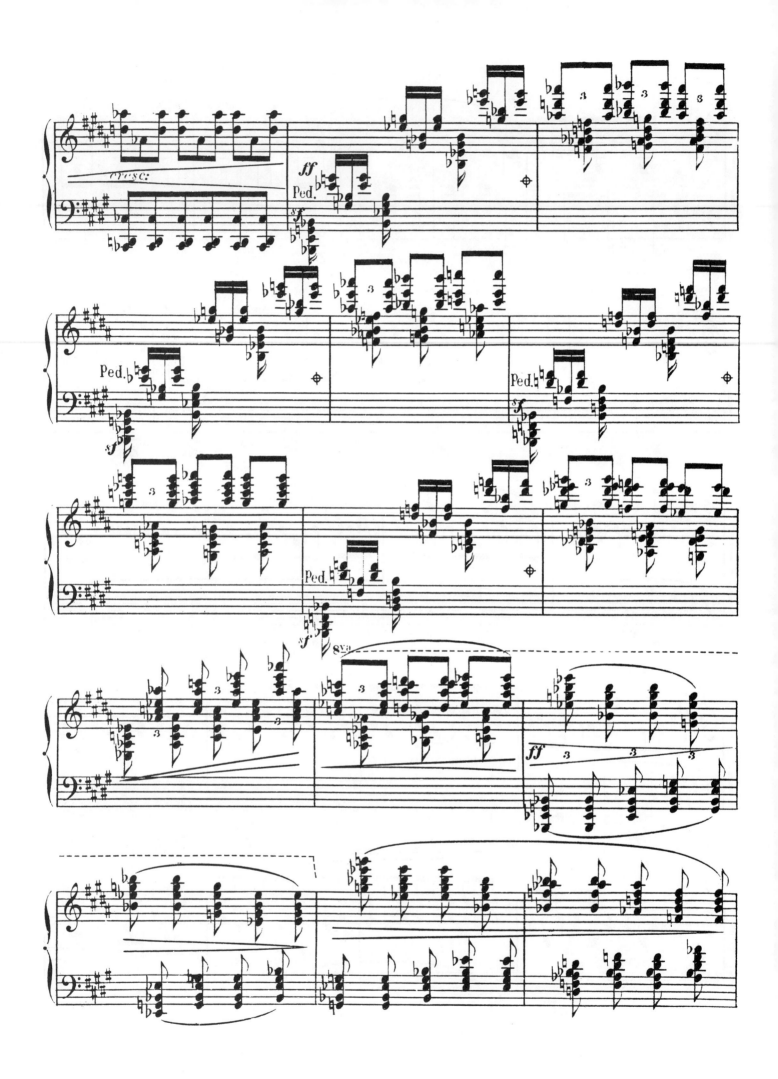

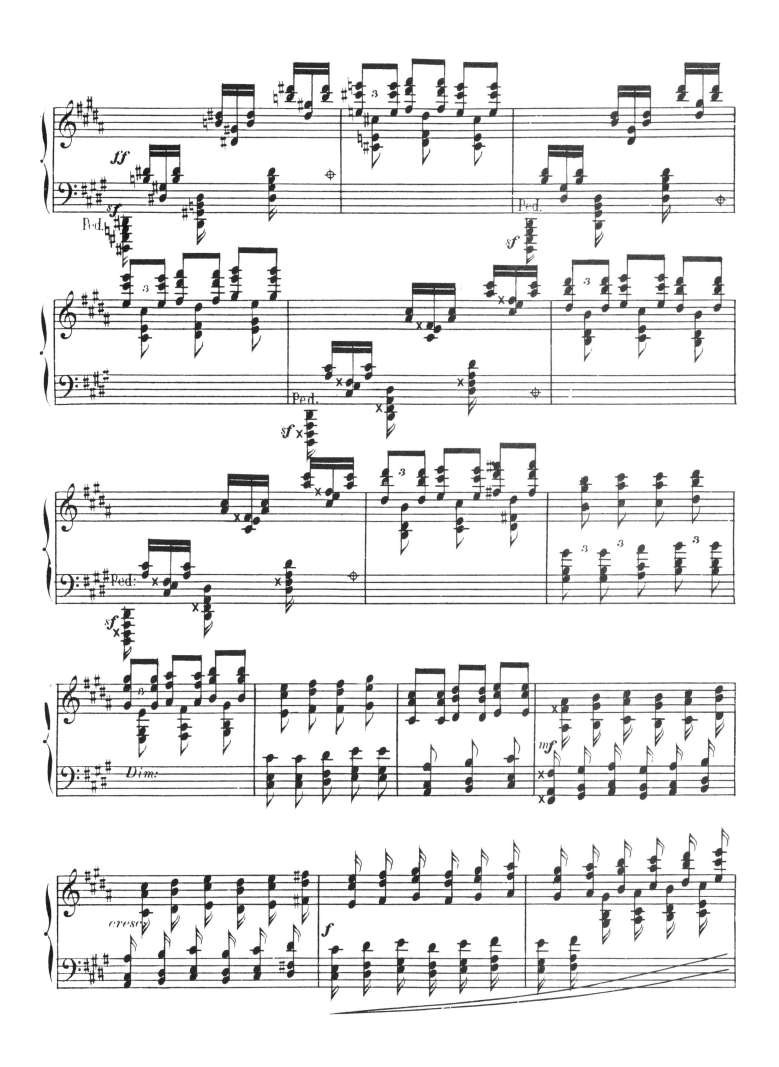

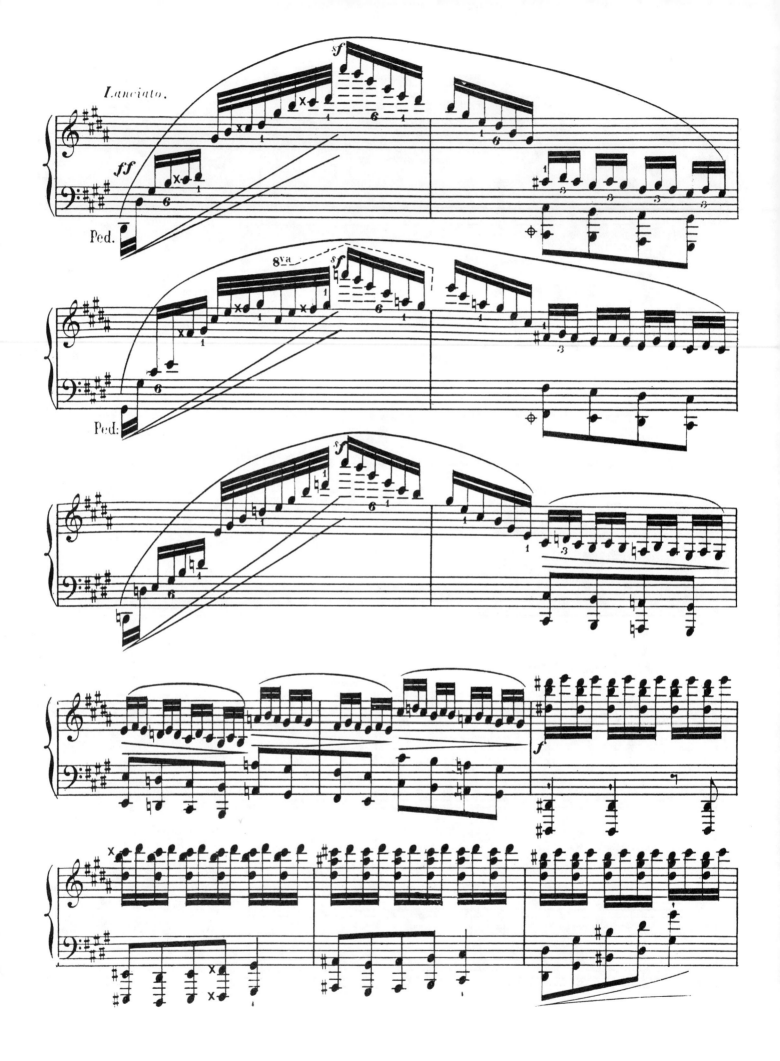

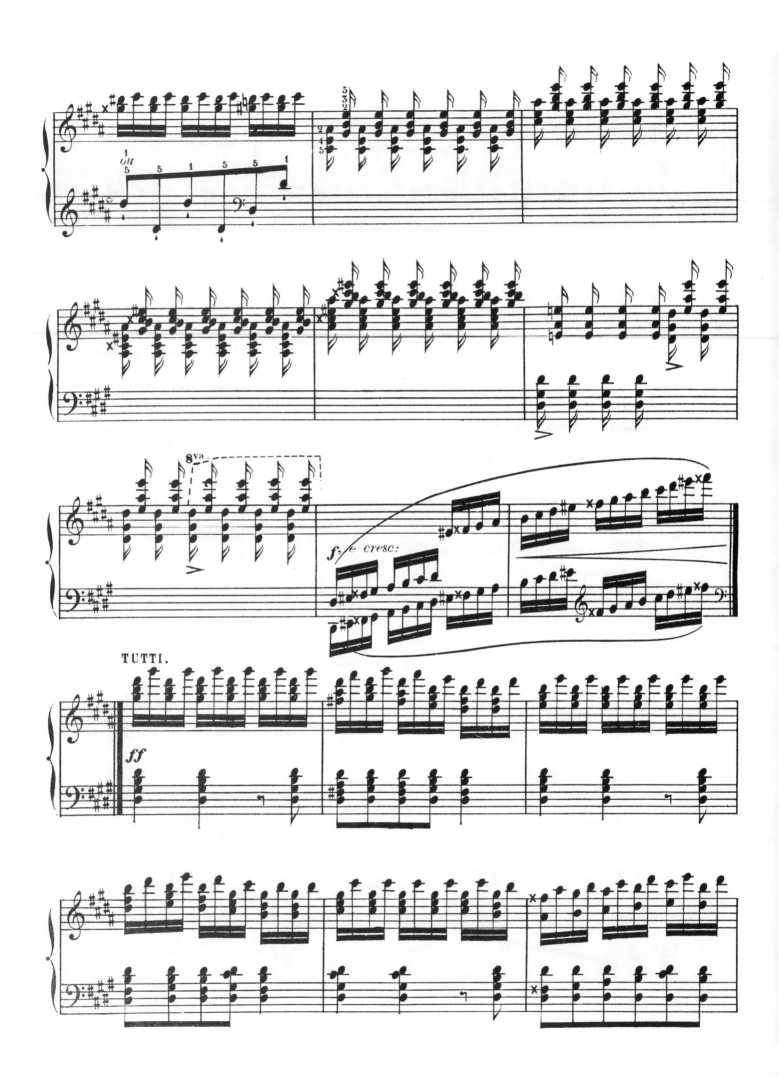

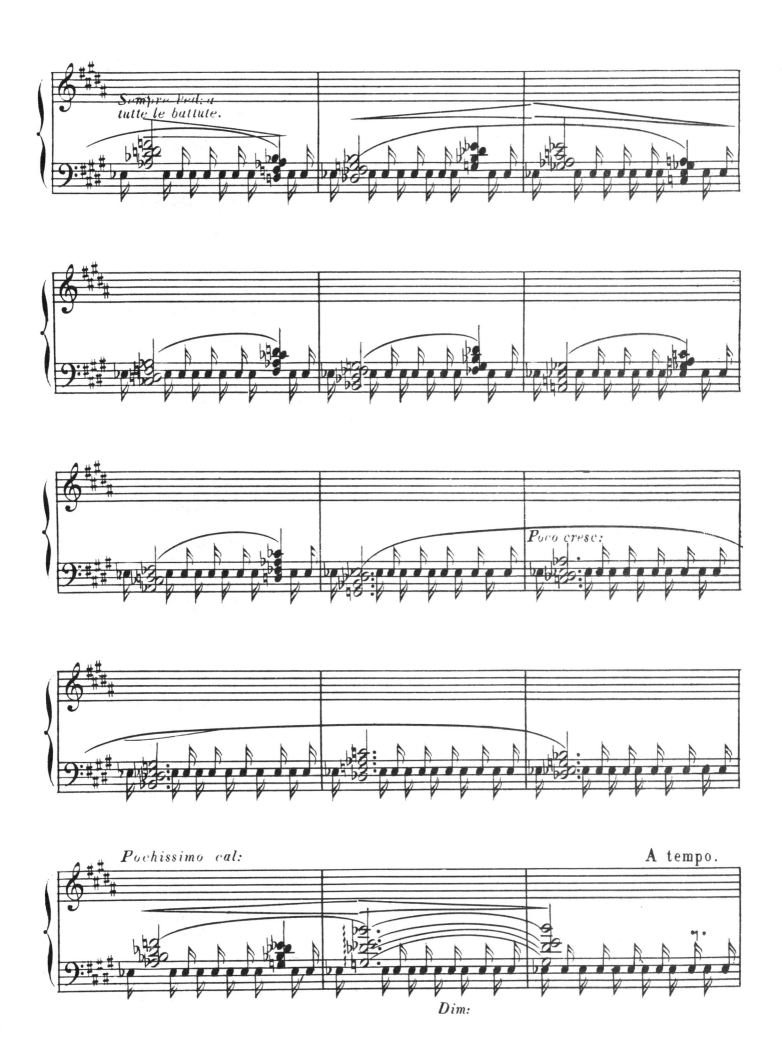

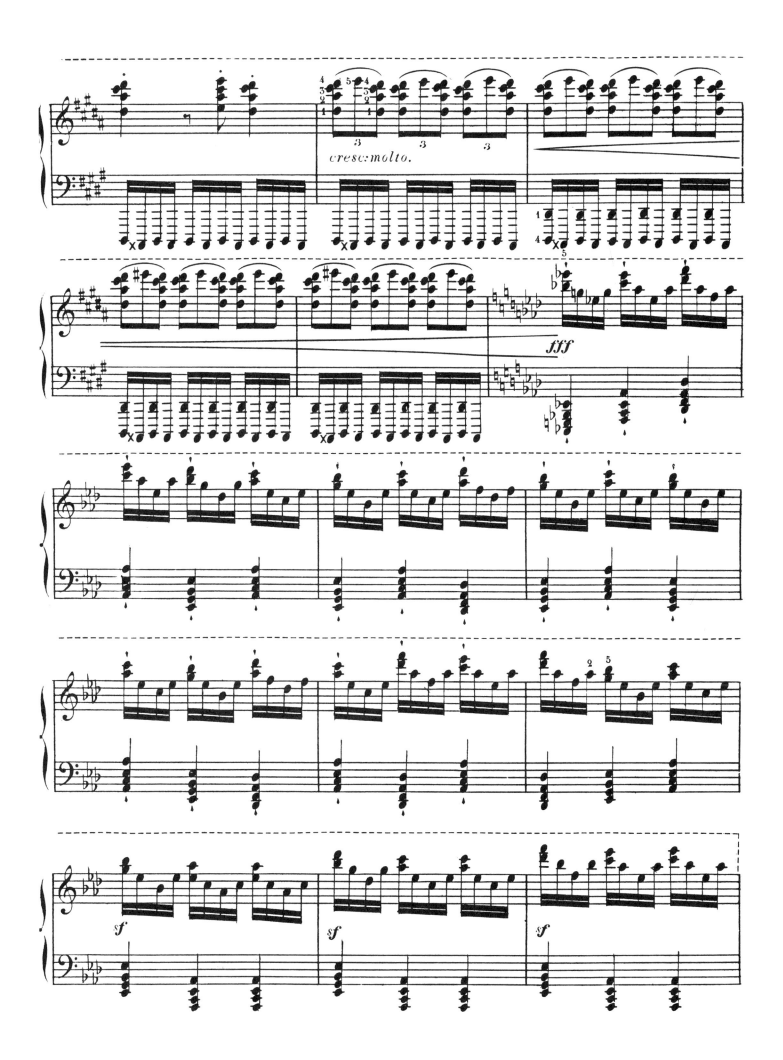

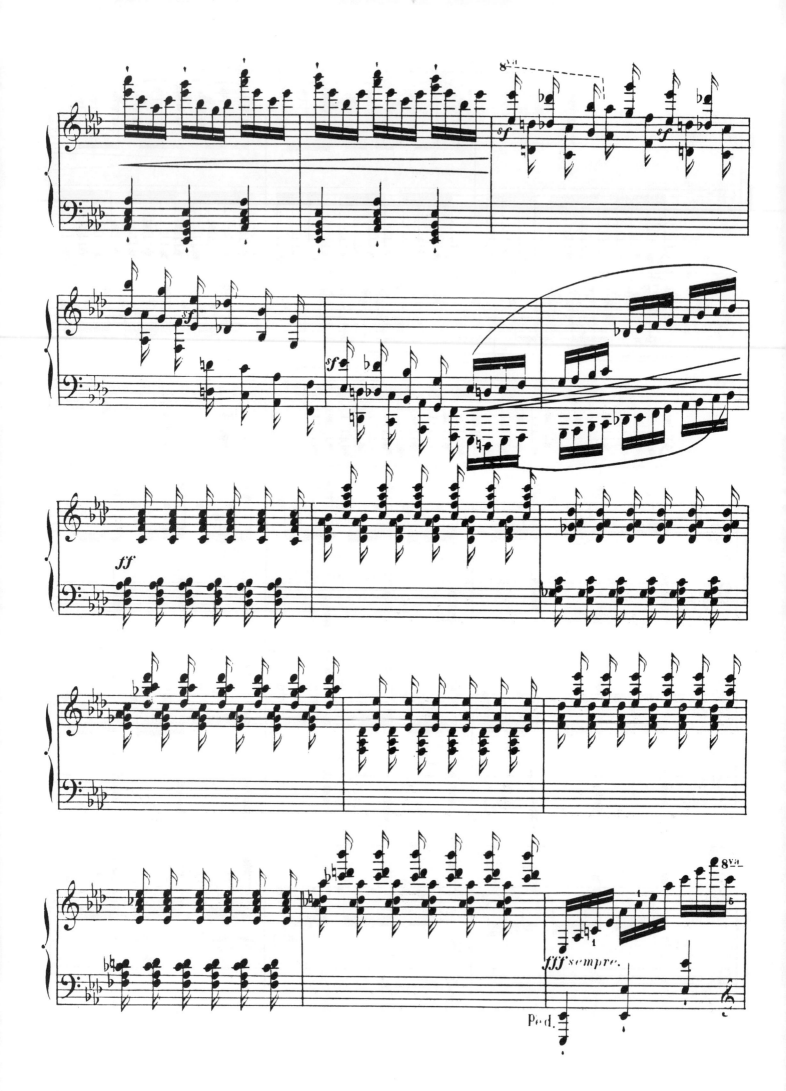

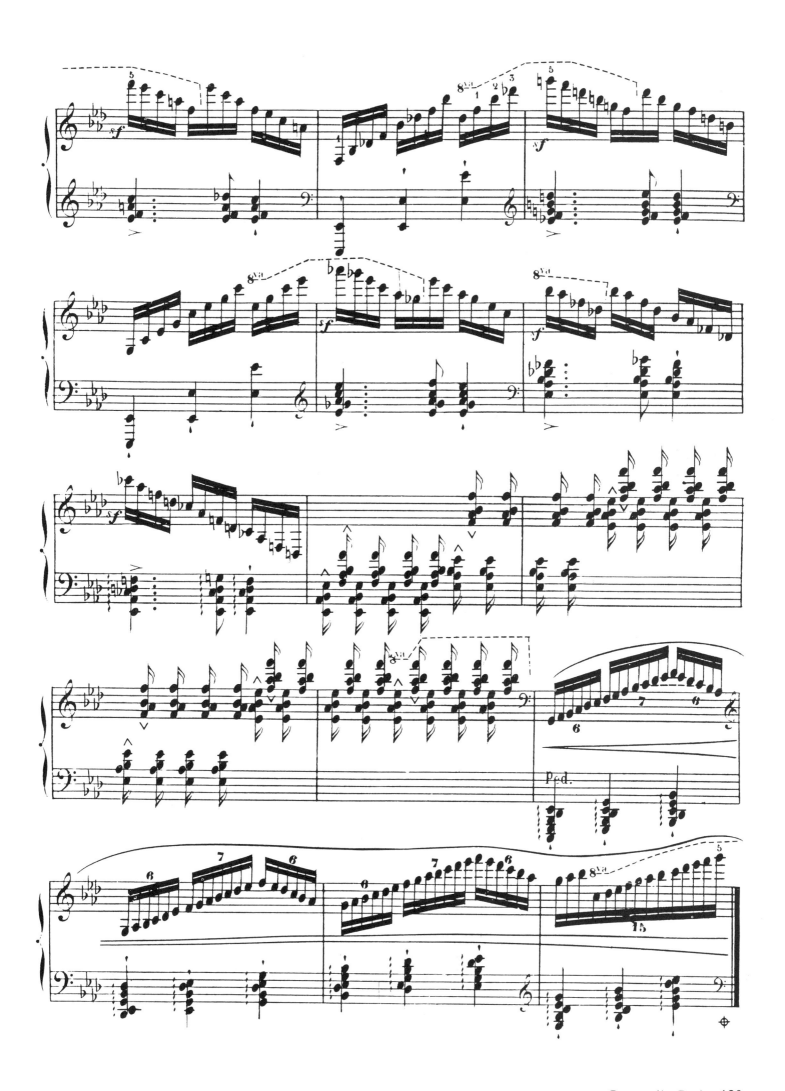

2nd Part
(Op. 39, No. 9)

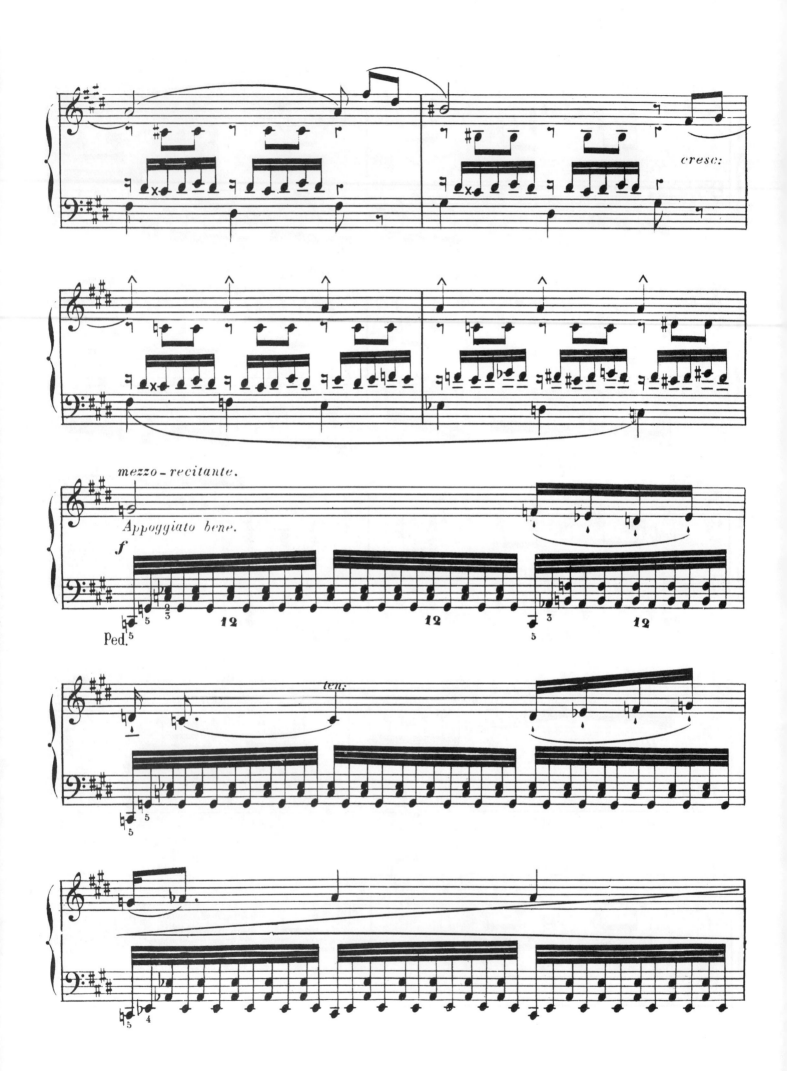

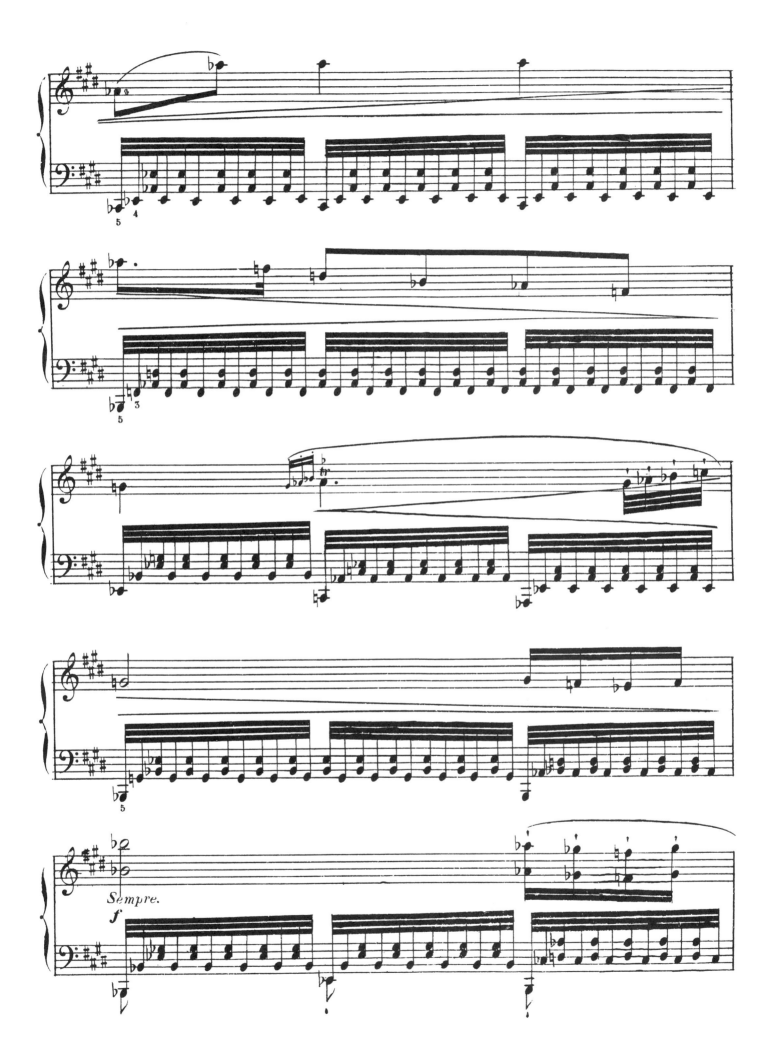

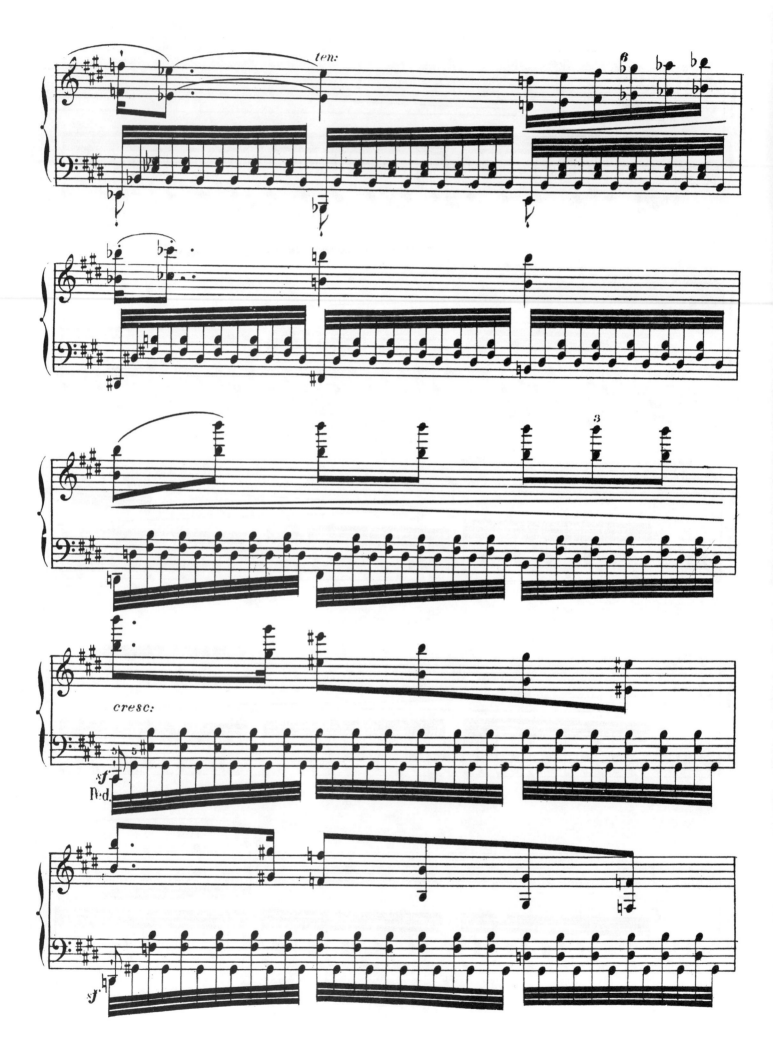

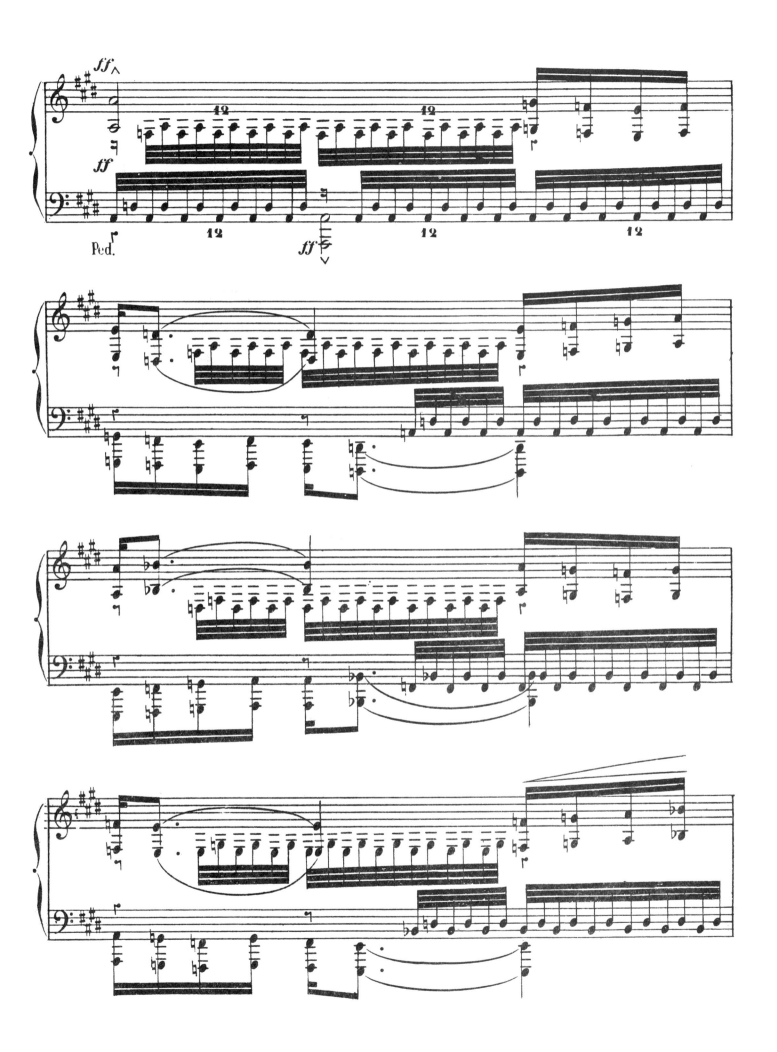

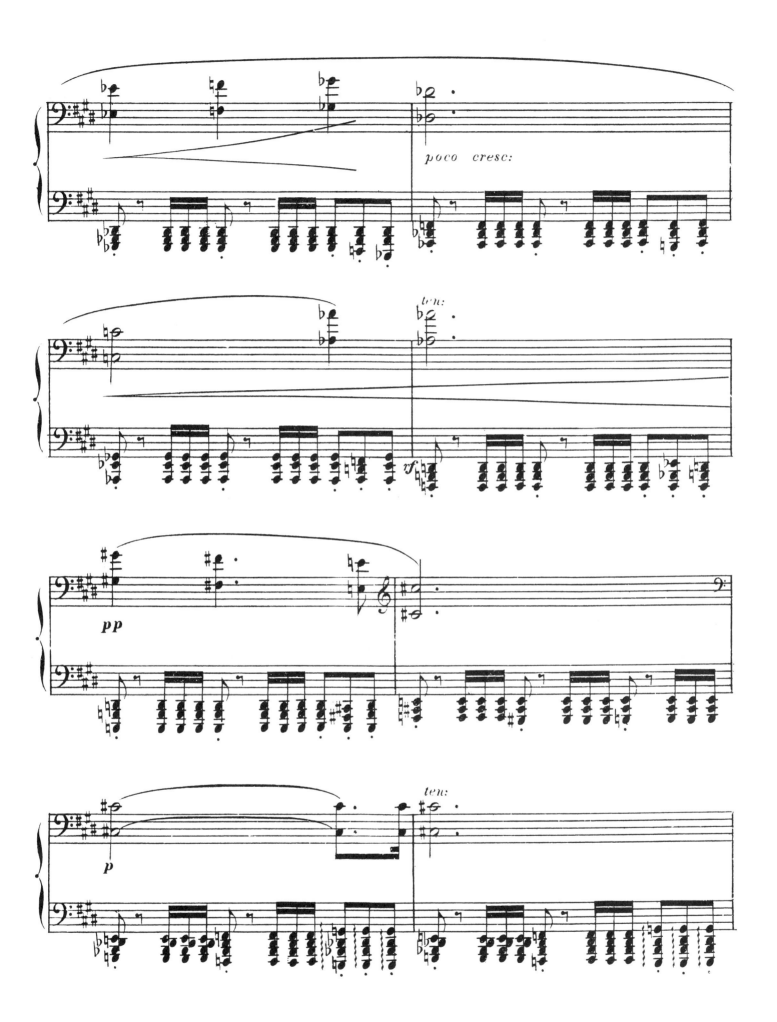

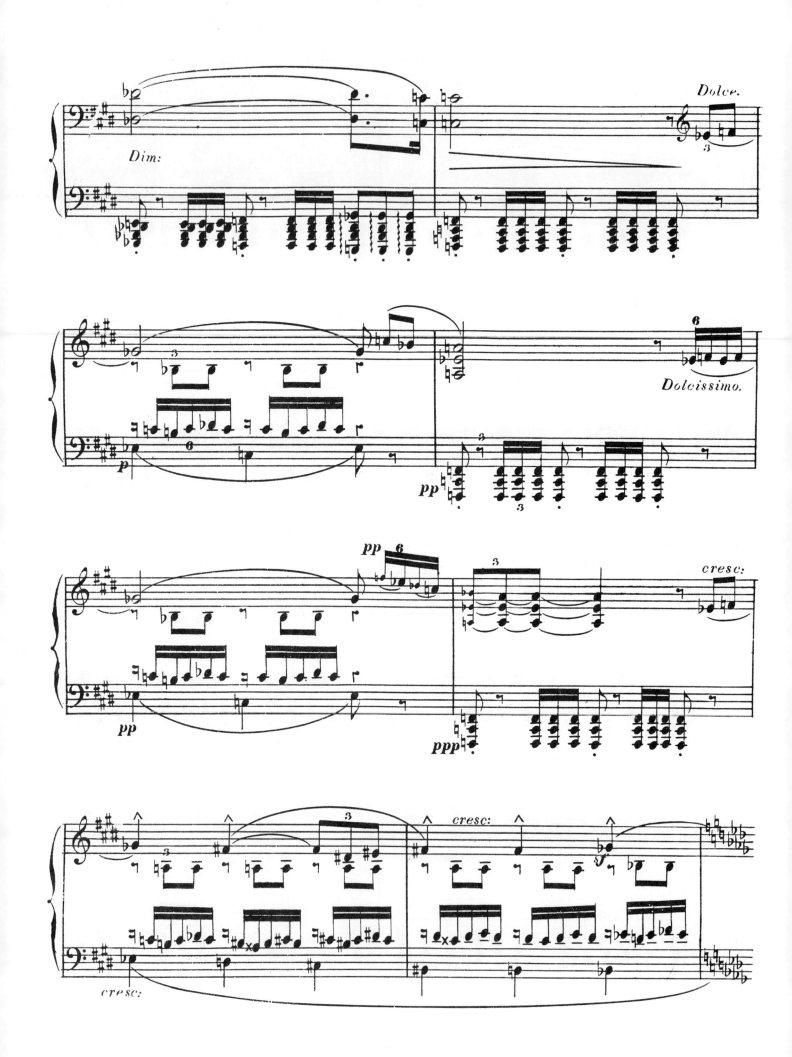

3rd Part
(Op. 39, No. 10)

Allegretto alla barbaresca (100 = ♩)

PIANO:

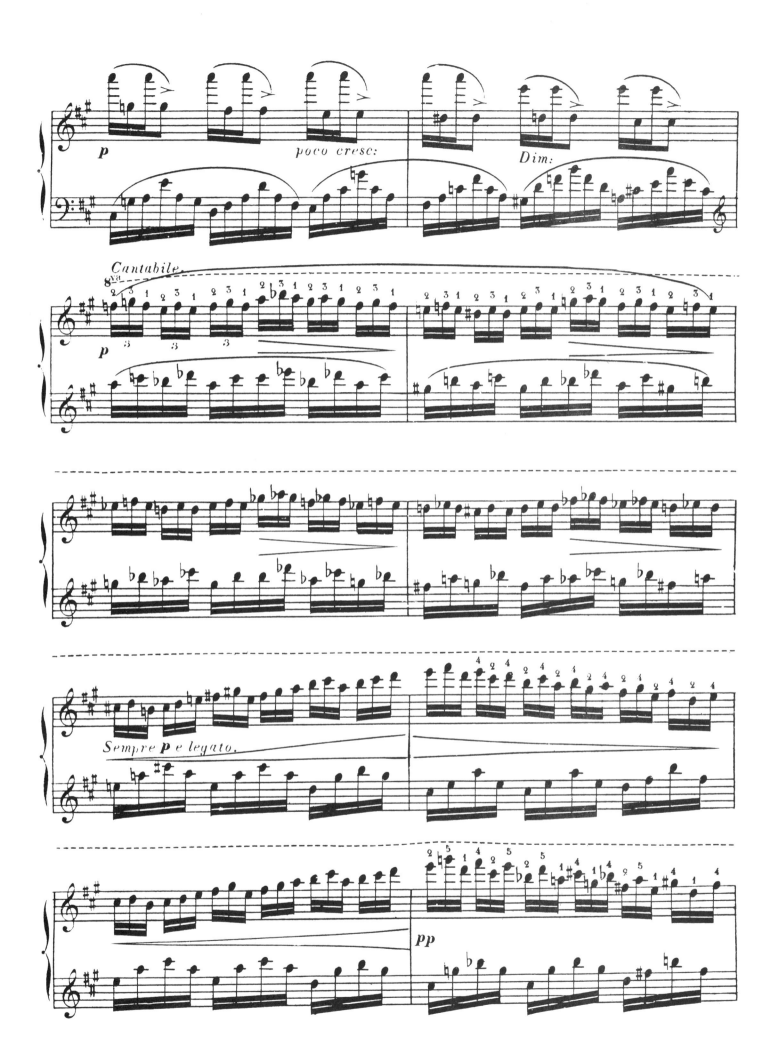

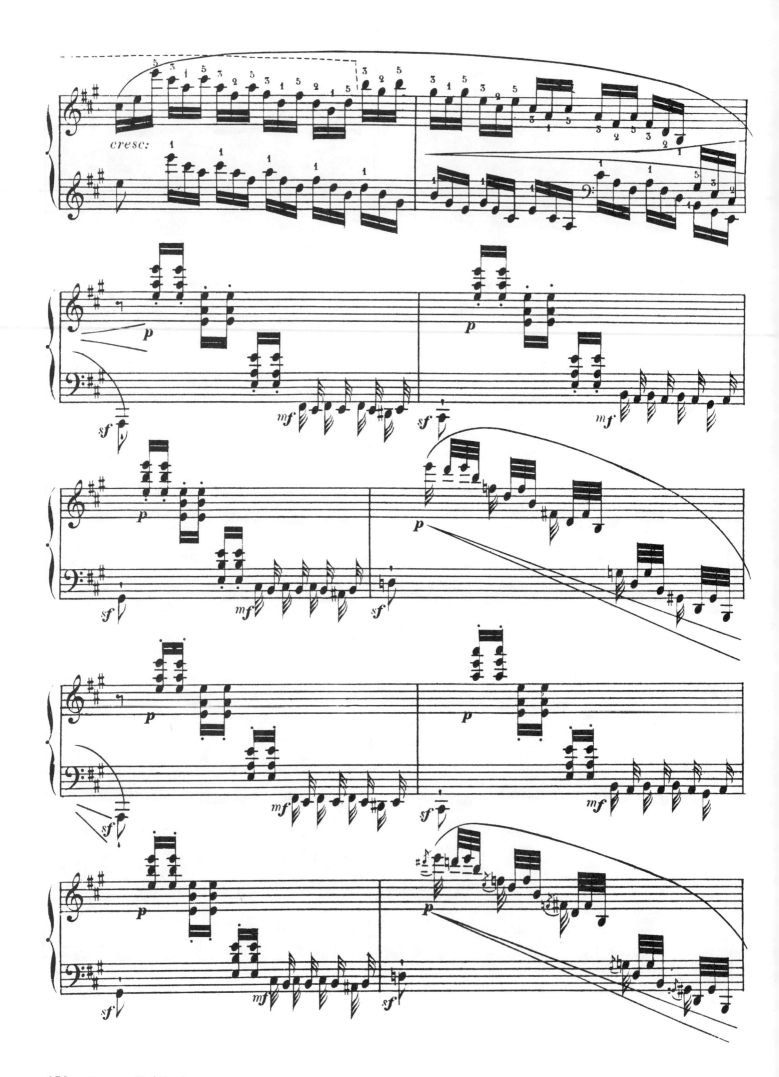

QUASI-SOLO.

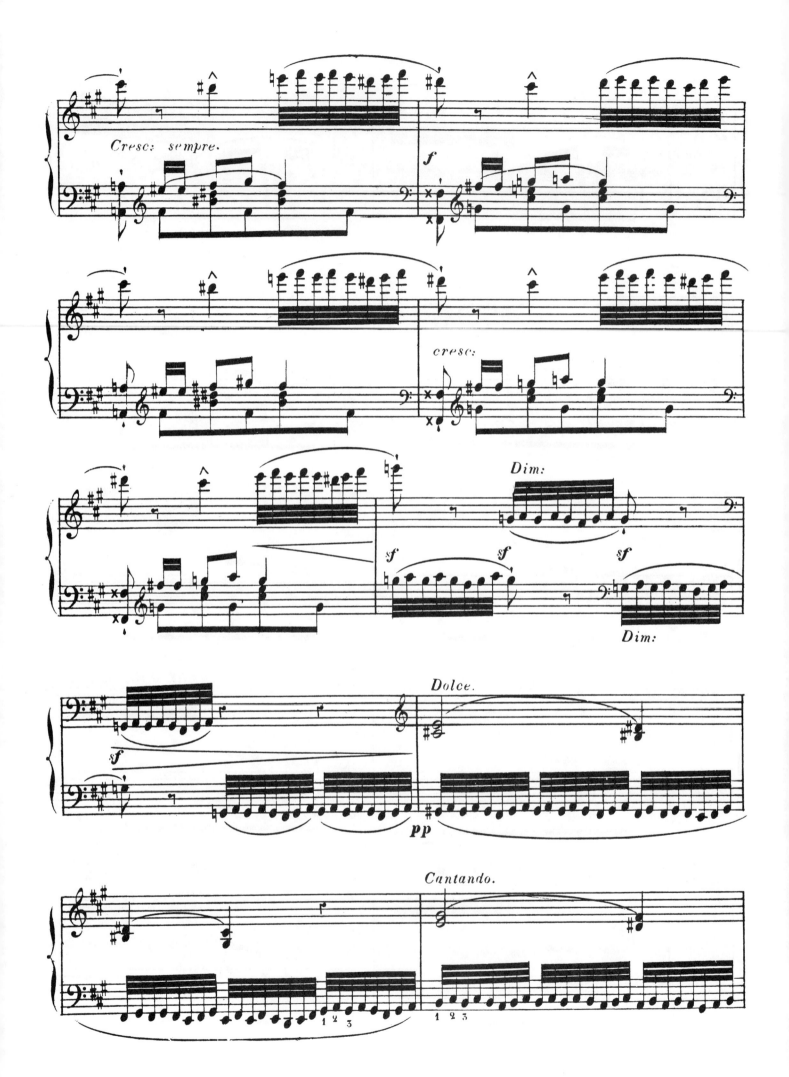

Un tantino poco più mosso.

Piano, legato e delicatamente.

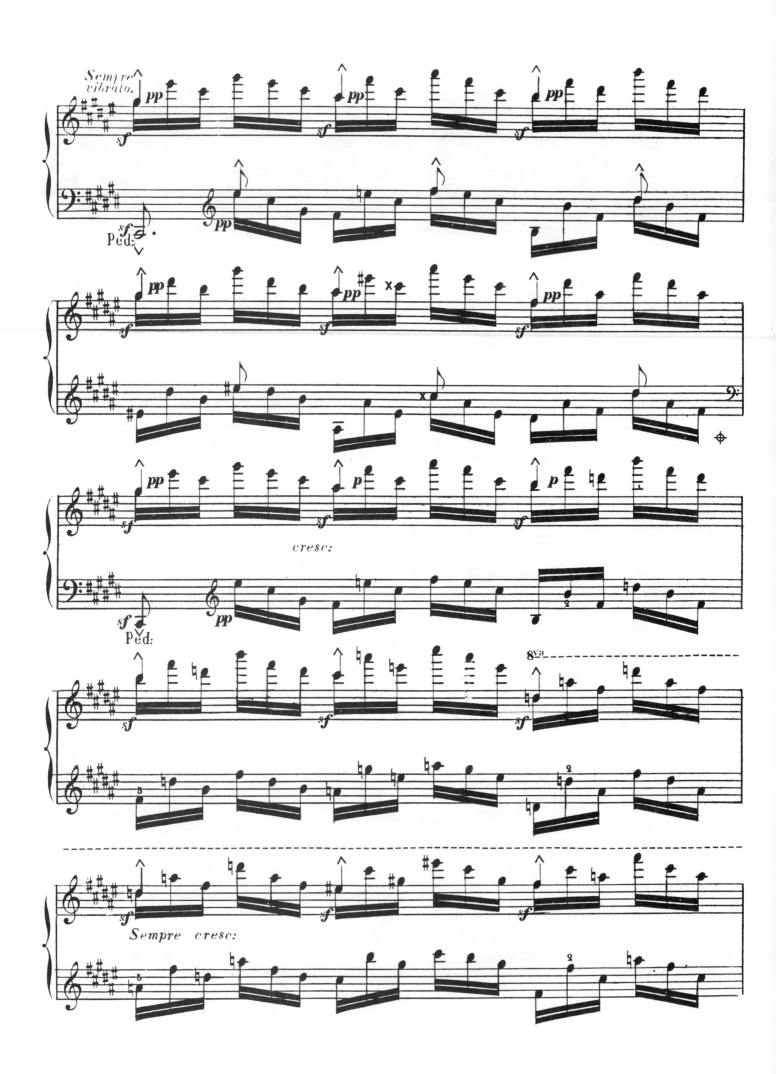

Le Festin d'Ésope

(Aesop's Feast)

Op. 39, No. 12

(1857)

Le Festin d'Ésope

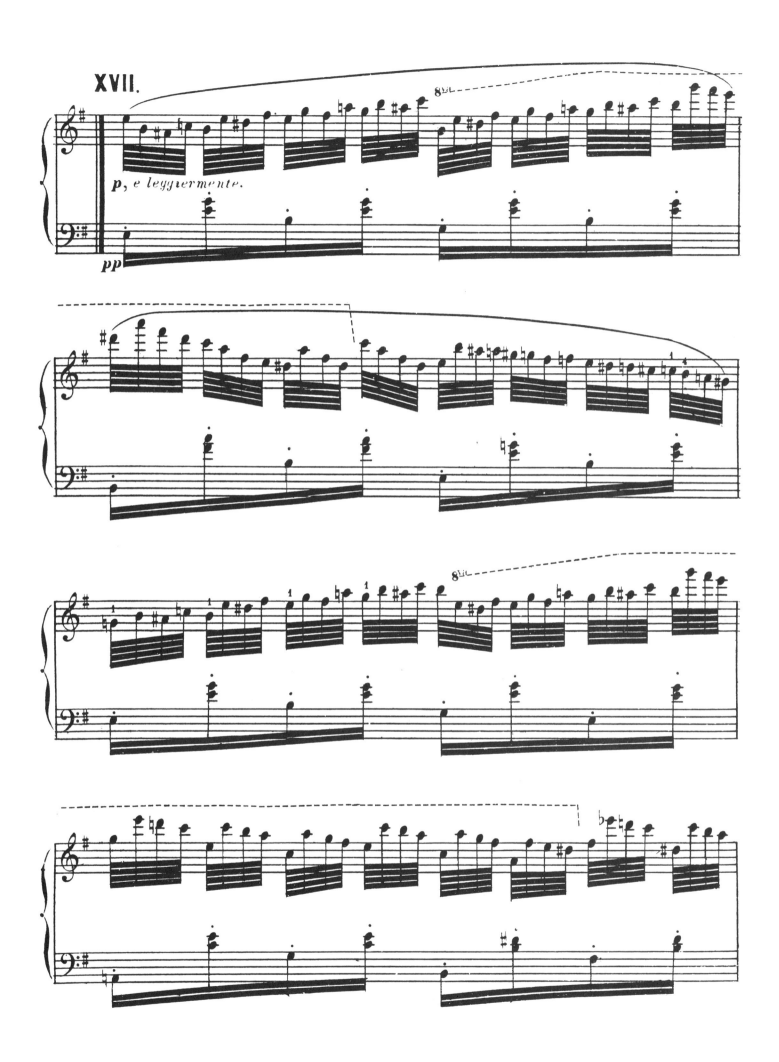

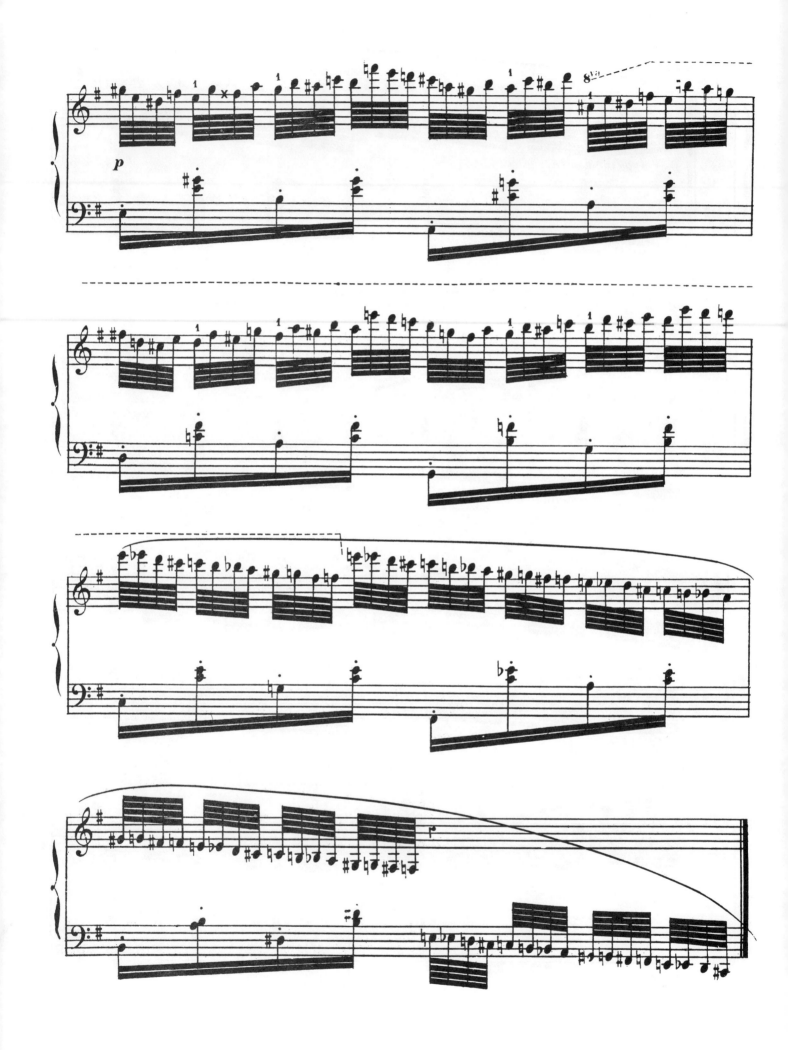

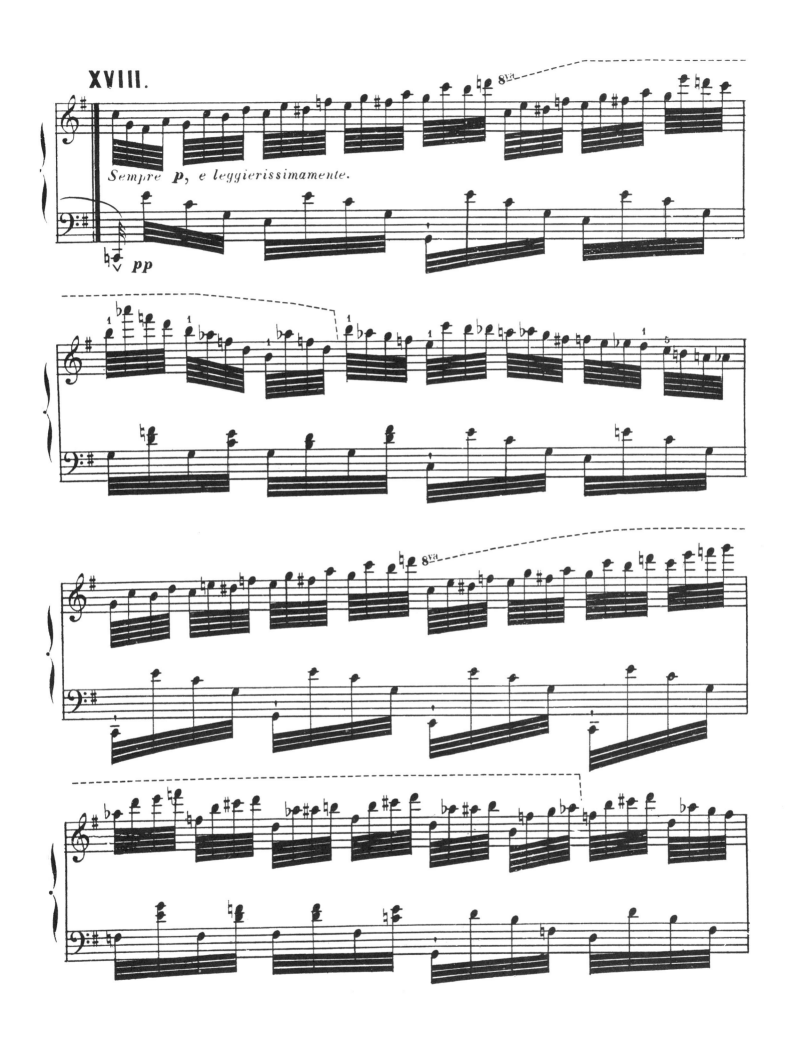

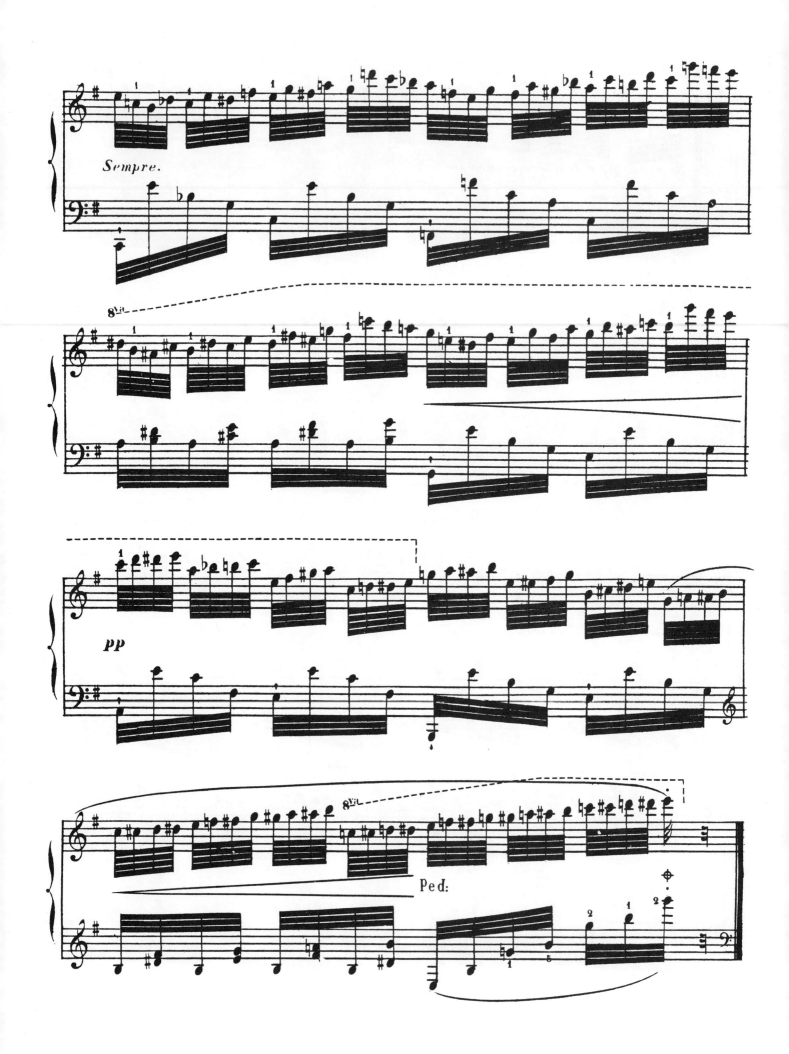

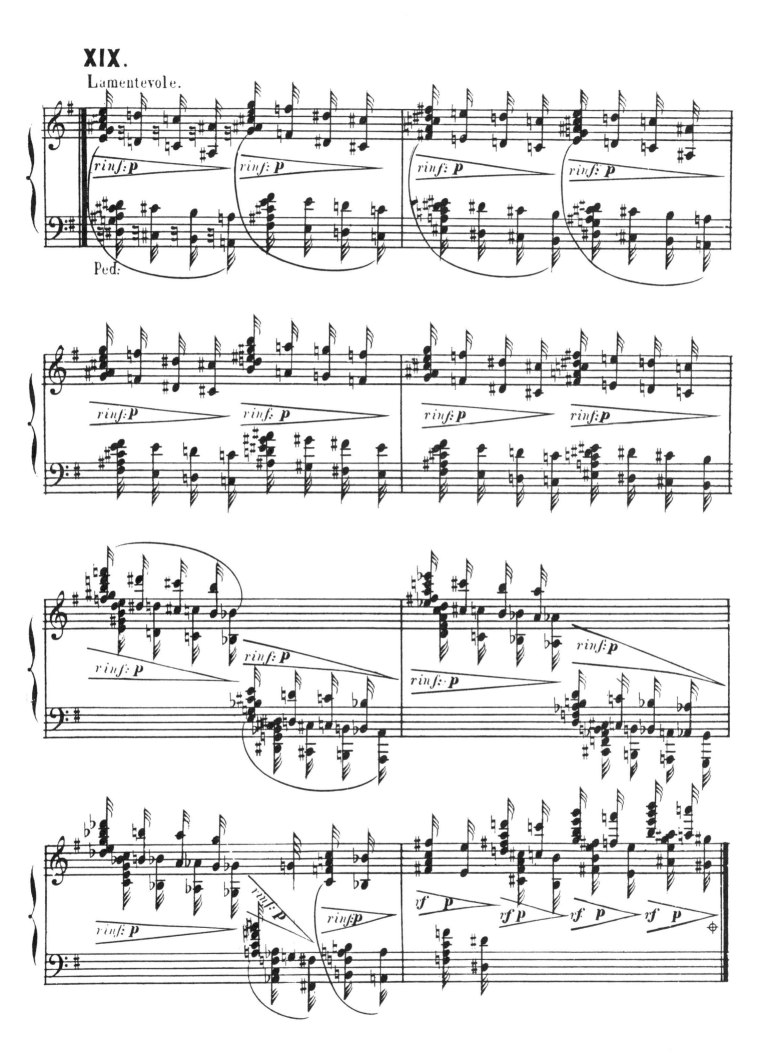

XXII.

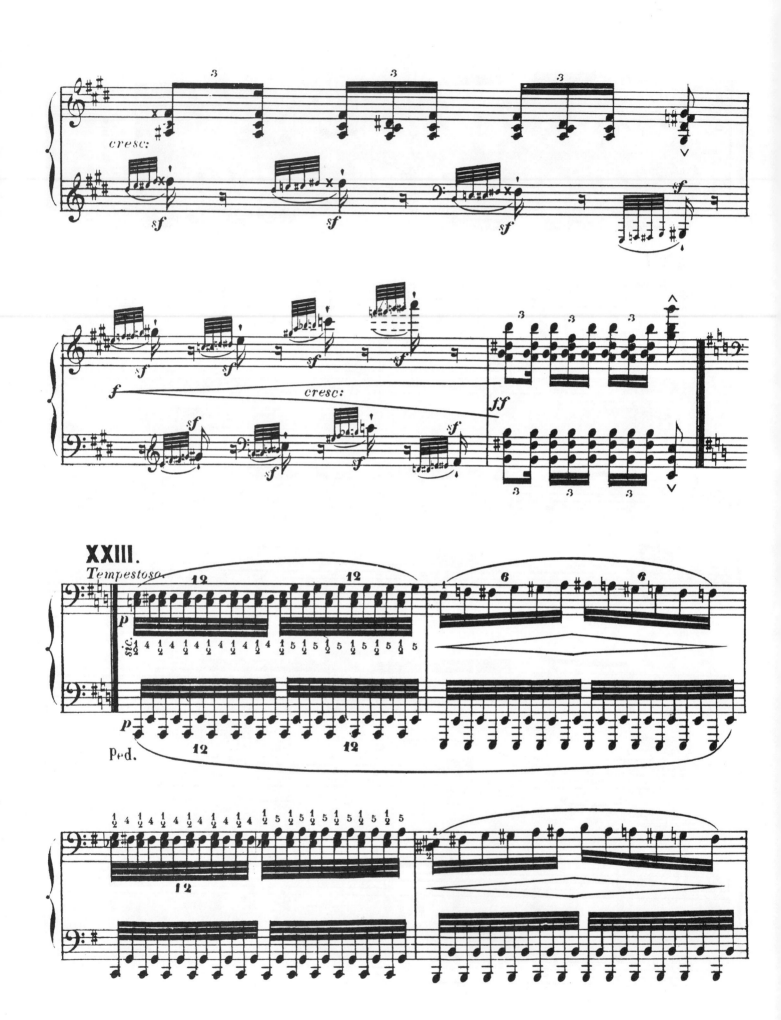

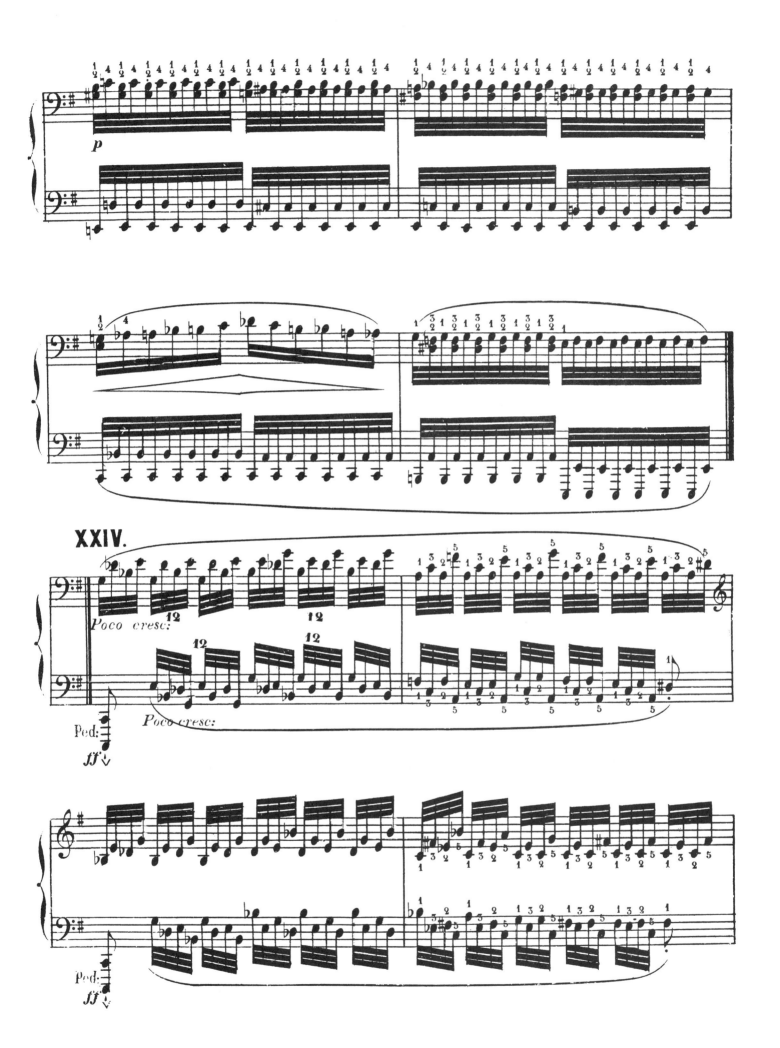

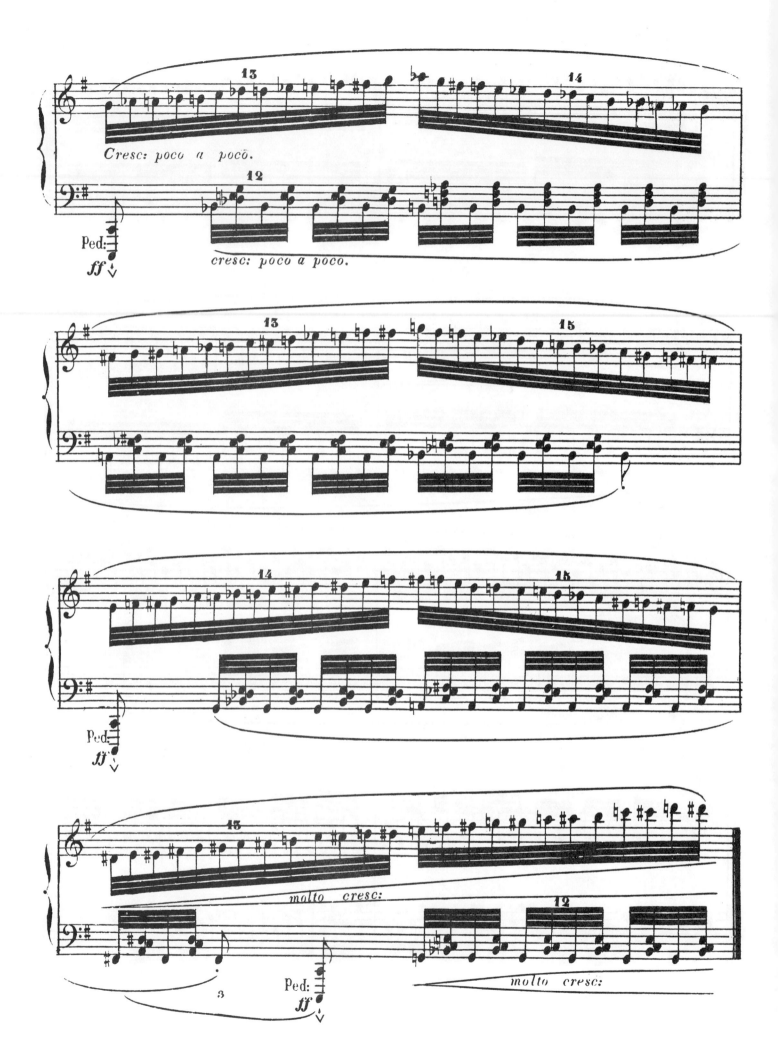

Saltarelle
Op. 23 (1844)

Barcarolle
Op. 65, No. 6 (ca. 1844)

Toccatina
Op. 75 (ca. 1872)

Saltarelle

Op. 23

Barcarolle

No. 6 from *Troisième Recueil de Chants* (Third Collection of Songs)

Op. 65

Assez lentement.

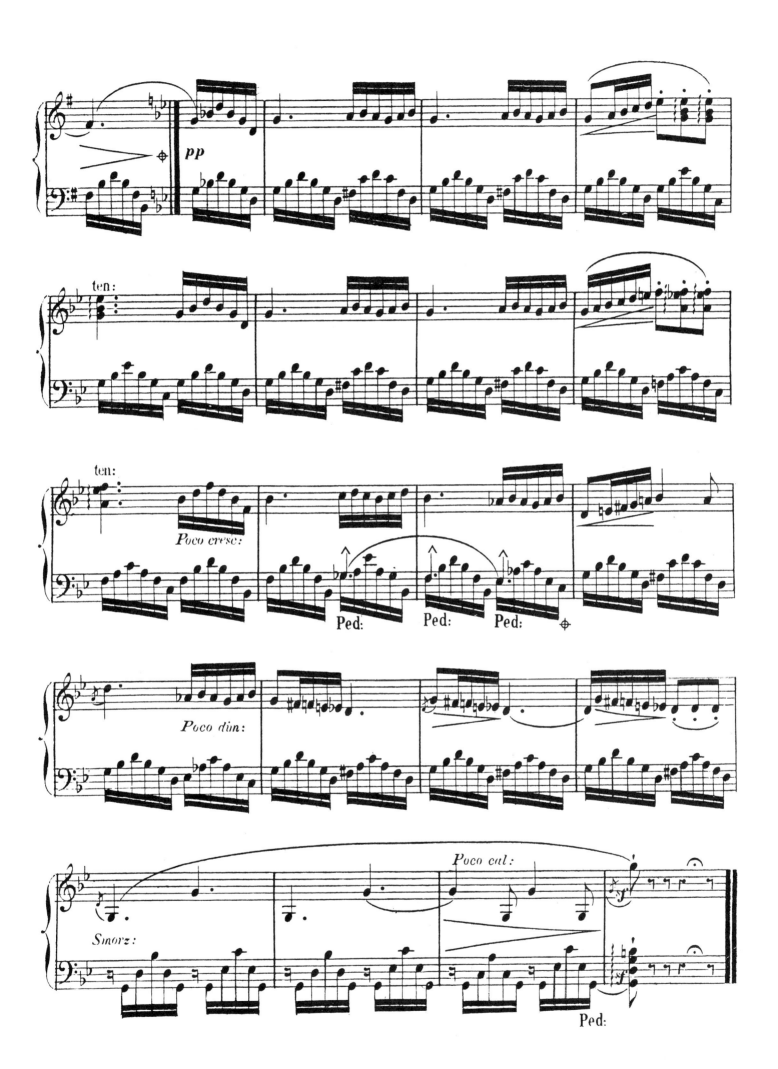

Toccatina
Op. 75

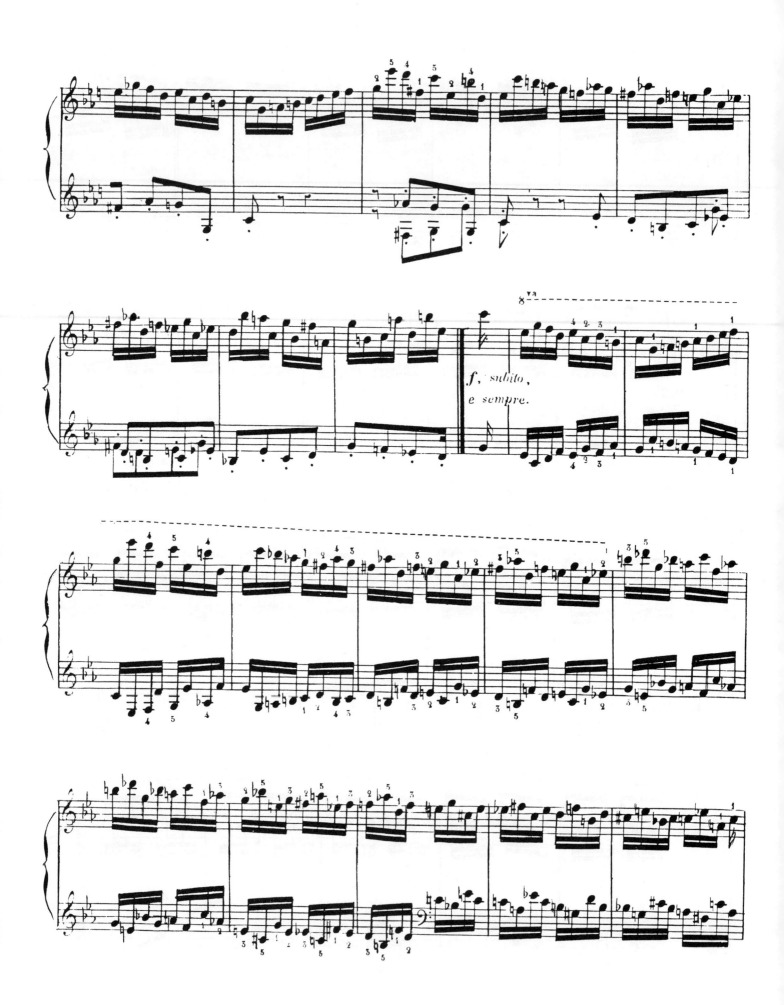

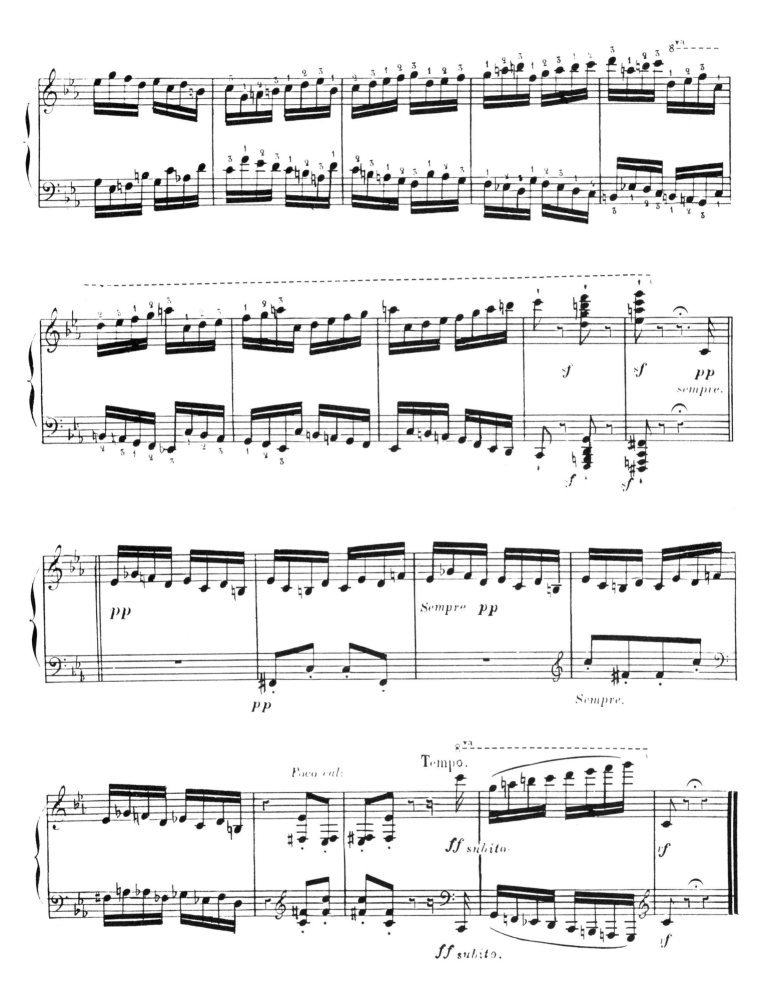

END OF EDITION

Dover Piano and Keyboard Editions

ORGAN WORKS, César Franck. Composer's best-known works for organ, including Six Pieces, Trois Pieces, and Trois Chorals. Oblong format for easy use at keyboard. Authoritative Durand edition. 208pp. 11⅜ × 8¼.
25517-4 Pa. **$13.95**

IBERIA AND ESPAÑA: Two Complete Works for Solo Piano, Isaac Albeniz. Spanish composer's greatest piano works in authoritative editions. Includes the popular "Tango." 192pp. 9 × 12. 25367-8 Pa. **$10.95**

GOYESCAS, SPANISH DANCES AND OTHER WORKS FOR SOLO PIANO, Enrique Granados. Great Spanish composer's most admired, most performed suites for the piano, in definitive Spanish editions. 176pp. 9 × 12. 25481-X Pa. **$9.95**

SELECTED PIANO COMPOSITIONS, César Franck, edited by Vincent d'Indy. Outstanding selection of influential French composer's piano works, including early pieces and the two masterpieces–Prelude, Choral and Fugue; and Prelude, Aria and Finale. Ten works in all. 138pp. 9 × 12. 23269-7 Pa. **$10.95**

THE COMPLETE PRELUDES AND ETUDES FOR PIANOFORTE SOLO, Alexander Scriabin. All the preludes and etudes including many perfectly spun miniatures. Edited by K. N. Igumnov and Y. I. Mil'shteyn. 250pp. 9 × 12. 22919-X Pa. **$11.95**

COMPLETE PIANO SONATAS, Alexander Scriabin. All ten of Scriabin's sonatas, reprinted from an authoritative early Russian edition. 256pp. 8⅜ × 11¼. 25850-5 Pa. **$12.95**

COMPLETE PRELUDES AND ETUDES-TABLEAUX, Serge Rachmaninoff. Forty-one of his greatest works for solo piano, including the riveting C Minor, G-Minor and B-Minor preludes, in authoritative editions. 208pp. 8⅜ × 11¼. 25696-0 Pa. **$11.95**

COMPLETE PIANO SONATAS, Sergei Prokofiev. Definitive Russian edition of nine sonatas (1907–1953), among the most important compositions in the modern piano repertoire. 288pp. 8⅜ × 11¼. (Available in U.S. only) 25689-8 Pa. **$12.95**

GYMNOPÉDIES, GNOSSIENNES AND OTHER WORKS FOR PIANO, Erik Satie. The largest Satie collection of piano works yet published, 17 in all, reprinted from the original French editions. 176pp. 9 × 12. (Not available in France or Germany) 25978-1 Pa. **$10.95**

TWENTY SHORT PIECES FOR PIANO (Sports et Divertissements), Erik Satie. French master's brilliant thumbnail sketches–verbal and musical–of various outdoor sports and amusements. English translations, 20 illustrations. Rare, limited 1925 edition. 48pp. 12 × 8⅞. (Not available in France or Germany) 24365-6 Pa. **$6.95**

COMPLETE PRELUDES, IMPROMPTUS AND VALSES-CAPRICES, Gabriel Fauré. Eighteen elegantly wrought piano works in authoritative editions. Only one-volume collection. 144pp. 9 × 12. (Not available in France or Germany) 25789-4 Pa. **$8.95**

PIANO MUSIC OF BÉLA BARTÓK, Series I, Béla Bartók. New, definitive Archive Edition incorporating composer's corrections. Includes *Funeral March* from *Kossuth, Fourteen Bagatelles,* Bartók's break to modernism. 167pp. 9 × 12. (Available in U.S. only) 24108-4 Pa. **$11.95**

PIANO MUSIC OF BÉLA BARTÓK, Series II, Béla Bartók. Second in the Archive Edition incorporating composer's corrections. 85 short pieces *For Children, Two Elegies, Two Romanian Dances,* etc. 192pp. 9 × 12. (Available in U.S. only) 24109-2 Pa. **$11.95**

FRENCH PIANO MUSIC, AN ANTHOLOGY, Isidor Phillipp (ed.). 44 complete works, 1670–1905, by Lully, Couperin, Rameau, Alkan, Saint-Saëns, Delibes, Bizet, Godard, many others; favorites, lesser-known examples, but all top quality. 188pp. 9 × 12. (Not available in France or Germany) 23381-2 Pa. **$12.95**

NINETEENTH-CENTURY EUROPEAN PIANO MUSIC: Unfamiliar Masterworks, John Gillespie (ed.). Difficult-to-find etudes, toccatas, polkas, impromptus, waltzes, etc., by Albéniz, Bizet, Chabrier, Fauré, Smetana, Richard Strauss, Wagner and 16 other composers. 62 pieces. 343pp. 9 × 12. (Not available in France or Germany) 23447-9 Pa. **$19.95**

RARE MASTERPIECES OF RUSSIAN PIANO MUSIC: Eleven Pieces by Glinka, Balakirev, Glazunov and Others, edited by Dmitry Feofanov. Glinka's *Prayer,* Balakirev's *Reverie,* Liapunov's *Transcendental Etude, Op. 11, No. 10,* and eight others–full, authoritative scores from Russian texts. 144pp. 9 × 12. 24659-0 Pa. **$9.95**

HUMORESQUES AND OTHER WORKS FOR SOLO PIANO, Antonín Dvořák. Humoresques, Op. 101, complete, Silhouettes, Op. 8, Poetic Tone Pictures, Theme with Variations, Op. 36, 4 Slavonic Dances, more. 160pp. 9 × 12. 28355-0 Pa. **$10.95**

PIANO MUSIC, Louis M. Gottschalk. 26 pieces (including covers) by early 19th-century American genius. "Bamboula," "The Banjo," other Creole, Negro-based material, through elegant salon music. 301pp. 9¼ × 12. 21683-7 Pa. **$15.95**

SOUSA'S GREAT MARCHES IN PIANO TRANSCRIPTION, John Philip Sousa. Playing edition includes: "The Stars and Stripes Forever," "King Cotton," "Washington Post," much more. 24 illustrations. 111pp. 9 × 12. 23132-1 Pa. **$7.95**

COMPLETE PIANO RAGS, Scott Joplin. All 38 piano rags by the acknowledged master of the form, reprinted from the publisher's original editions complete with sheet music covers. Introduction by David A. Jasen. 208pp. 9 × 12. 25807-6 Pa. **$9.95**

RAGTIME REDISCOVERIES, selected by Trebor Jay Tichenor. 64 unusual rags demonstrate diversity of style, local tradition. Original sheet music. 320pp. 9 × 12. 23776-1 Pa. **$14.95**

RAGTIME RARITIES, edited by Trebor Jay Tichenor. 63 tuneful, rediscovered piano rags by 51 composers (or teams). Does not duplicate selections in *Classic Piano Rags* (Dover, 20469-3). 305pp. 9 × 12. 23157-7 Pa. **$14.95**

CLASSIC PIANO RAGS, selected with an introduction by Rudi Blesh. Best ragtime music (1897–1922) by Scott Joplin, James Scott, Joseph F. Lamb, Tom Turpin, nine others. 364pp. 9 × 12. 20469-3 Pa. **$15.95**

RAGTIME GEMS: Original Sheet Music for 25 Ragtime Classics, edited by David A. Jasen. Includes original sheet music and covers for 25 rags, including three of Scott Joplin's finest: *Searchlight Rag, Rose Leaf Rag* and *Fig Leaf Rag.* 122pp. 9 × 12. 25248-5 Pa. **$8.95**

NOCTURNES AND BARCAROLLES FOR SOLO PIANO, Gabriel Fauré. 12 nocturnes and 12 barcarolles reprinted from authoritative French editions. 208pp. 9⅜ × 12¼. (Not available in France or Germany) 27955-3 Pa. **$12.95**

FAVORITE WALTZES, POLKAS AND OTHER DANCES FOR SOLO PIANO, Johann Strauss, Jr. Blue Danube, Tales from Vienna Woods, many other best-known waltzes and other dances. 160pp. 9 × 12. 27851-4 Pa. **$10.95**

SELECTED PIANO WORKS FOR FOUR HANDS, Franz Schubert. 24 separate pieces (16 most popular titles): Three Military Marches, Lebensstürme, Four Polonaises, Four Ländler, etc. Rehearsal numbers added. 273pp. 9 × 12. 23529-7 Pa. **$12.95**

Available from your music dealer or write for free Music Catalog to
Dover Publications, Inc., Dept. MUBI, 31 East 2nd Street, Mineola, N.Y. 11501.

Dover Piano and Keyboard Editions

SHORTER WORKS FOR PIANOFORTE SOLO, Franz Schubert. All piano music except Sonatas, Dances, and a few unfinished pieces. Contains Wanderer, Impromptus, Moments Musicals, Variations, Scherzi, etc. Breitkopf and Härtel edition. 199pp. 9⅜ × 12¼. 22648-4 Pa. **$11.95**

WALTZES AND SCHERZOS, Frédéric Chopin. All of the Scherzos and nearly all (20) of the Waltzes from the authoritative Mikuli edition. Editorial commentary. 160pp. 9 × 12. 24316-8 Pa. **$9.95**

COMPLETE PRELUDES AND ETUDES FOR SOLO PIANO, Frédéric Chopin. All 25 Preludes, all 27 Etudes by greatest composer of piano music. Authoritative Mikuli edition. 192pp. 9 × 12. 24052-5 Pa. **$8.95**

COMPLETE BALLADES, IMPROMPTUS AND SONATAS, Frédéric Chopin. The four Ballades, four Impromptus and three Sonatas. Authoritative Paderewski edition. 240pp. 9 × 12. (Available in U.S. only) 24164-5 Pa. **$10.95**

NOCTURNES AND POLONAISES, Frédéric Chopin. 20 *Nocturnes* and 11 *Polonaises* reproduced from the authoritative Mikuli edition for pianists, students, and musicologists. Commentary. 224pp. 9 × 12. 24564-0 Pa. **$10.95**

COMPLETE MAZURKAS, Frédéric Chopin. 51 best-loved compositions, reproduced directly from the authoritative Kistner edition edited by Carl Mikuli. 160pp. 9 × 12. 25548-4 Pa. **$8.95**

FANTASY IN F MINOR, BARCAROLLE, BERCEUSE AND OTHER WORKS FOR SOLO PIANO, Frédéric Chopin. 15 works, including one of the greatest of the Romantic period, the Fantasy in F Minor, Op. 49, reprinted from the authoritative German edition prepared by Chopin's student, Carl Mikuli. 224pp. 8⅝ × 11¼. 25950-1 Pa. **$7.95**

COMPLETE HUNGARIAN RHAPSODIES FOR SOLO PIANO, Franz Liszt. All 19 Rhapsodies reproduced directly from an authoritative Russian edition. All headings, footnotes translated to English. Best one volume edition available. 224pp. 8⅝ × 11¼. 24744-9 Pa. **$11.95**

ANNÉES DE PÈLERINAGE, COMPLETE, Franz Liszt. Authoritative Russian edition of piano masterpieces: *Première Année (Suisse): Deuxième Année (Italie)* and *Venezia e Napoli; Troisième Année,* other related pieces. 288pp. 9⅜ × 12¼. 25627-8 Pa. **$13.95**

COMPLETE ETUDES FOR SOLO PIANO, Series I: Including the Transcendental Etudes, Franz Liszt, edited by Busoni. Also includes Etude in 12 Exercises, 12 Grandes Etudes and Mazeppa. Breitkopf & Härtel edition. 272pp. 8⅝ × 11¼. 25815-7 Pa. **$12.95**

COMPLETE ETUDES FOR SOLO PIANO, Series II: Including the Paganini Etudes and Concert Etudes, Franz Liszt, edited by Busoni. Also includes Morceau de Salon, Ab Irato. Breitkopf & Härtel edition. 192pp. 8⅝ × 11¼. 25816-5 Pa. **$9.95**

SONATA IN B MINOR AND OTHER WORKS FOR PIANO, Franz Liszt. One of Liszt's most performed piano masterpieces, with the six Consolations, ten *Harmonies poetiques et religieuses,* two Ballades and two Legendes. Breitkopf & Härtel edition. 208pp. 8⅝ × 11¼. 26182-4 Pa. **$9.95**

PIANO TRANSCRIPTIONS FROM FRENCH AND ITALIAN OPERAS, Franz Liszt. Virtuoso transformations of themes by Mozart, Verdi, Bellini, other masters, into unforgettable music for piano. Published in association with American Liszt Society. 247pp. 9 × 12. 24273-0 Pa. **$13.95**

MEPHISTO WALTZ AND OTHER WORKS FOR SOLO PIANO, Franz Liszt. Rapsodie Espagnole, Liebestraüme Nos. 1–3, Valse Oubliée No. 1, Nuages Gris, Polonaises Nos. 1 and 2, Grand Galop Chromatique, more. 192pp. 8⅜ × 11¼. 28147-7 Pa. **$10.95**

COMPLETE WORKS FOR PIANOFORTE SOLO, Felix Mendelssohn. Breitkopf and Härtel edition of Capriccio in F# Minor, Sonata in E Major, Fantasy in F# Minor, Three Caprices, Songs without Words, and 20 other works. Total of 416pp. 9⅜ × 12¼. Two-vol. set. 23136-4, 23137-2 Pa. **$23.90**

COMPLETE SONATAS AND VARIATIONS FOR SOLO PIANO, Johannes Brahms. All sonatas, five variations on themes from Schumann, Paganini, Handel, etc. Vienna Gesellschaft der Musikfreunde edition. 178pp. 9 × 12. 22650-6 Pa. **$10.95**

COMPLETE SHORTER WORKS FOR SOLO PIANO, Johannes Brahms. All solo music not in other two volumes. Waltzes, Scherzo in E Flat Minor, Eight Pieces, Rhapsodies, Fantasies, Intermezzi, etc. Vienna Gesellschaft der Musikfreunde. 180pp. 9 × 12. 22651-4 Pa. **$10.95**

COMPLETE TRANSCRIPTIONS, CADENZAS AND EXERCISES FOR SOLO PIANO, Johannes Brahms. Vienna Gesellschaft der Musikfreunde edition, vol. 15. Studies after Chopin, Weber, Bach; gigues, sarabandes; 10 Hungarian dances, etc. 178pp. 9 × 12. 22652-2 Pa. **$10.95**

PIANO MUSIC OF ROBERT SCHUMANN, Series I, edited by Clara Schumann. Major compositions from the period 1830–39; *Papillons,* Toccata, Grosse Sonate No. 1, *Phantasiestücke, Arabeske, Blumenstück,* and nine other works. Reprinted from Breitkopf & Härtel edition. 274pp. 9⅜ × 12¼. 21459-1 Pa. **$13.95**

PIANO MUSIC OF ROBERT SCHUMANN, Series II, edited by Clara Schumann. Major compositions from period 1838–53; *Humoreske, Novelletten,* Sonate No. 2, 43 *Clavierstücke für die Jugend,* and six other works. Reprinted from Breitkopf & Härtel edition. 272pp. 9⅜ × 12¼. 21461-3 Pa. **$13.95**

PIANO MUSIC OF ROBERT SCHUMANN, Series III, edited by Clara Schumann. All solo music not in other two volumes, including *Symphonic Etudes, Phantaisie,* 13 other choice works. Definitive Breitkopf & Härtel edition. 224pp. 9⅜ × 12¼. 23906-3 Pa. **$11.95**

PIANO MUSIC 1888–1905, Claude Debussy. Deux Arabesques, Suite Bergamesque, Masques, first series of Images, etc. Nine others, in corrected editions. 175pp. 9⅜ × 12¼. 22771-5 Pa. **$8.95**

COMPLETE PRELUDES, Books 1 and 2, Claude Debussy. 24 evocative works that reveal the essence of Debussy's genius for musical imagery, among them many of the composer's most famous piano compositions. Glossary of French terms. 128pp. 8⅜ × 11¼. 25970-6 Pa. **$7.95**

PRELUDES, BOOK I: The Autograph Score, Claude Debussy. Superb facsimile reproduced directly from priceless autograph score in Pierpont Morgan Library in New York. New Introduction by Roy Howat. 48pp. 8⅜ × 11. 25549-2 Pa. **$8.95**

PIANO MASTERPIECES OF MAURICE RAVEL, Maurice Ravel. Handsome affordable treasury; *Pavane pour une infante defunte, jeux d'eau, Sonatine, Miroirs,* more. 128pp. 9 × 12. (Not available in France or Germany) 25137-3 Pa. **$8.95**

COMPLETE LYRIC PIECES FOR PIANO, Edvard Grieg. All 66 pieces from Grieg's ten sets of little mood pictures for piano, favorites of generations of pianists. 224pp. 9⅜ × 12¼. 26176-X Pa. **$11.95**

Available from your music dealer or write for ***free*** *Music Catalog to*
Dover Publications, Inc., Dept. MUBI, 31 East 2nd Street, Mineola, N.Y. 11501.

Dover Piano and Keyboard Editions

THE WELL-TEMPERED CLAVIER: Books I and II, Complete, Johann Sebastian Bach. All 48 preludes and fugues in all major and minor keys. Authoritative Bach-Gesellschaft edition. Explanation of ornaments in English, tempo indications, music corrections. 208pp. 9⅜ × 12¼.
24532-2 Pa. **$9.95**

KEYBOARD MUSIC, J. S. Bach. Bach-Gesellschaft edition. For harpsichord, piano, other keyboard instruments. English Suites, French Suites, Six Partitas, Goldberg Variations, Two-Part Inventions, Three-Part Sinfonias. 312pp. 8⅛ × 11. 22360-4 Pa. **$12.95**

ITALIAN CONCERTO, CHROMATIC FANTASIA AND FUGUE AND OTHER WORKS FOR KEYBOARD, Johann Sebastian Bach. Sixteen of Bach's best-known, most-performed and most-recorded works for the keyboard, reproduced from the authoritative Bach-Gesellschaft edition. 112pp. 9 × 12. 25387-2 Pa. **$8.95**

COMPLETE KEYBOARD TRANSCRIPTIONS OF CONCERTOS BY BAROQUE COMPOSERS, Johann Sebastian Bach. Sixteen concertos by Vivaldi, Telemann and others, transcribed for solo keyboard instruments. Bach-Gesellschaft edition. 128pp. 9⅜ × 12¼.
25529-8 Pa. **$9.95**

ORGAN MUSIC, J. S. Bach. Bach-Gesellschaft edition. 93 works. 6 Trio Sonatas, German Organ Mass, Orgelbüchlein, Six Schubler Chorales, 18 Choral Preludes. 357pp. 8⅛ × 11. 22359-0 Pa. **$13.95**

COMPLETE PRELUDES AND FUGUES FOR ORGAN, Johann Sebastian Bach. All 25 of Bach's complete sets of preludes and fugues (i.e. compositions written as pairs), from the authoritative Bach-Gesellschaft edition. 168pp. 8⅜ × 11. 24816-X Pa. **$10.95**

TOCCATAS, FANTASIAS, PASSACAGLIA AND OTHER WORKS FOR ORGAN, J. S. Bach. Over 20 best-loved works including Toccata and Fugue in D Minor, BWV 565; Passacaglia and Fugue in C Minor, BWV 582, many more. Bach-Gesellschaft edition. 176pp. 9 × 12.
25403-8 Pa. **$10.95**

TWO- AND THREE-PART INVENTIONS, J. S. Bach. Reproduction of original autograph ms. Edited by Eric Simon. 62pp. 8⅛ × 11.
21982-8 Pa. **$8.95**

THE 36 FANTASIAS FOR KEYBOARD, Georg Philipp Telemann. Graceful compositions by 18th-century master. 1923 Breslauer edition. 80pp. 8⅛ × 11. 25365-1 Pa. **$6.95**

GREAT KEYBOARD SONATAS, Carl Philipp Emanuel Bach. Comprehensive two-volume edition contains 51 sonatas by second, most important son of Johann Sebastian Bach. Originality, rich harmony, delicate workmanship. Authoritative French edition. Total of 384pp. 8⅜ × 11¼.
Series I 24853-4 Pa. **$11.95**
Series II 24854-2 Pa. **$10.95**

KEYBOARD WORKS/Series One: Ordres I–XIII; Series Two: Ordres XIV–XXVII and Miscellaneous Pieces, François Couperin. Over 200 pieces. Reproduced directly from edition prepared by Johannes Brahms and Friedrich Chrysander. Total of 496pp. 8⅛ × 11.
Series I 25795-9 Pa. **$10.95**
Series II 25796-7 Pa. **$11.95**

KEYBOARD WORKS FOR SOLO INSTRUMENTS, G. F. Handel. 35 neglected works from Handel's vast oeuvre, originally jotted down as improvisations. Includes Eight Great Suites, others. New sequence. 174pp. 9⅜ × 12¼. 24338-9 Pa. **$10.95**

WORKS FOR ORGAN AND KEYBOARD, Jan Pieterszoon Sweelinck. Nearly all of early Dutch composer's difficult-to-find keyboard works. Chorale variations; toccatas, fantasias; variations on secular, dance tunes. Also, incomplete and/or modified works, plus fantasia by John Bull. 272pp. 9 × 12. 24935-2 Pa. **$14.95**

ORGAN WORKS, Dietrich Buxtehude. Complete organ works of extremely influential pre-Bach composer. Toccatas, preludes, chorales, more. Definitive Breitkopf & Härtel edition. 320pp. 8⅜ × 11¼. (Available in U.S. only) 25682-0 Pa. **$14.95**

THE FUGUES ON THE MAGNIFICAT FOR ORGAN OR KEYBOARD, Johann Pachelbel. 94 pieces representative of Pachelbel's magnificent contribution to keyboard composition; can be played on the organ, harpsichord or piano. 100pp. 9 × 12. (Available in U.S. only)
25037-7 Pa. **$8.95**

MY LADY NEVELLS BOOKE OF VIRGINAL MUSIC, William Byrd. 42 compositions in modern notation from 1591 ms. For any keyboard instrument. 245pp. 8⅛ × 11. 22246-2 Pa. **$13.95**

ELIZABETH ROGERS HIR VIRGINALL BOOKE, edited with calligraphy by Charles J. F. Cofone. All 112 pieces from noted 1656 manuscript, most never before published. Composers include Thomas Brewer, William Byrd, Orlando Gibbons, etc. 125pp. 9 × 12. 23138-0 Pa. **$10.95**

THE FITZWILLIAM VIRGINAL BOOK, edited by J. Fuller Maitland, W. B. Squire. Famous early 17th-century collection of keyboard music, 300 works by Morley, Byrd, Bull, Gibbons, etc. Modern notation. Total of 938pp. 8⅜ × 11. Two-vol. set. 21068-5, 21069-3 Pa. **$34.90**

GREAT KEYBOARD SONATAS, Series I and Series II, Domenico Scarlatti. 78 of the most popular sonatas reproduced from the G. Ricordi edition edited by Alessandro Longo. Total of 320pp. 8⅜ × 11¼.
Series I 24996-4 Pa. **$9.95**
Series II 25003-2 Pa. **$9.95**

COMPLETE PIANO SONATAS, Joseph Haydn. 52 sonatas reprinted from authoritative Breitkopf & Härtel edition. Extremely clear and readable; ample space for notes, analysis. 464pp. 9⅜ × 12¼. 24726-0 Pa. **$11.95**
24727-9 Pa. **$11.95**

BAGATELLES, RONDOS AND OTHER SHORTER WORKS FOR PIANO, Ludwig van Beethoven. Most popular and most performed shorter works, including Rondo a capriccio in G and Andante in F. Breitkopf & Härtel edition. 128pp. 9⅜ × 12¼. 25392-9 Pa. **$8.95**

COMPLETE VARIATIONS FOR SOLO PIANO, Ludwig van Beethoven. Contains all 21 sets of Beethoven's piano variations, including the extremely popular *Diabelli Variations, Op. 120.* 240pp. 9⅜ × 12¼.
25188-8 Pa. **$12.95**

COMPLETE PIANO SONATAS, Ludwig van Beethoven. All sonatas in fine Schenker edition, with fingering, analytical material. One of best modern editions. 615pp. 9 × 12. Two-vol. set. 23134-8, 23135-6 Pa. **$25.90**

COMPLETE SONATAS FOR PIANOFORTE SOLO, Franz Schubert. All 15 sonatas. Breitkopf and Härtel edition. 293pp. 9⅜ × 12¼.
22647-6 Pa. **$13.95**

DANCES FOR SOLO PIANO, Franz Schubert. Over 350 waltzes, minuets, landler, ecossaises, other charming, melodic dance compositions reprinted from the authoritative Breitkopf & Härtel edition. 192pp. 9⅜ × 12¼.
26107-7 Pa. **$11.95**

Available from your music dealer or write for ***free*** *Music Catalog to*
Dover Publications, Inc., Dept. MUBI, 31 East 2nd Street, Mineola, N.Y. 11501.